LATE HAVE I LOVED YOU

PART-TIME PRIESTLY FORMATION FOR MATURE ADULTS: PSYCHO-SPIRITUAL ASPECTS

Matthias J.A. Ham (Ed.)

Original Dutch: *Laat heb ik U liefgekregen, priesteropleiding van volwassenen in deeltijd, psychospirituele aspecten.*

Matt Ham (red.)

2007, Ten Have, Baarn.

© 2011 English Edition, Lulu Press

ISBN 978-0-557-63920-5

Matthias J.A. Ham, all rights reserved

Translations: Fr. Dr. Jan Snijders, Marist (NL)

Revisions: The Rev. Dr. Alan Le Grys (UK), The Rev. Dr. Han van den Blink (USA)

Photo Shepherd: Kashmir India, 2006 © Thomas Bauwens,

Author: padrematthias@uol.com.br

With special thanks and gratitude for the friendship
and for the enormous amount of work done,
without which the English edition would not have
been possible, to:

Fr. Dr. Jan Snijders, Marist (NL)
The Rev. Dr. Alan Le Grys (UK)
The Rev. Dr. Han van den Blink (USA)

Because of their vast experience in training
future priests they understood exactly
what I wanted to say and helped
the English edition become
a faithful translation
of the original Dutch text

FOREWORD

It is a pleasure to commend to you a book that deals with part-time priestly formation for mature adults who feel called to take on the ministry of priest or deacon in the Roman Catholic Church while still exercising a profession or holding an ordinary job 'in the world'.

The Bovendonk programme was begun in 1983 with the intention of opening a pathway to ministry in the Church to candidates for whom this would otherwise be impossible. It would widen access to the Church's ministry in a specific and new way. After a few years experience, this model of formation was given an additional dimension: candidates coming from a secular career who wish to follow this path were provided with a formation tailored to meet their specific needs, in which scholarship and practical pastoral placements are central, but to which they themselves contribute through their own life-experience. In this way, they are assisted and supported as they make the transition from secular work to the environment of the Church.

This book considers various aspects of the formation process which have been developed specifically for this purpose. It shows that official Church documents encourage the development of a specific type of formation for such candidates. It tells us of different attempts to formulate an appropriate programme, and how these attempts influenced each other. We learn that tailored formation of this kind is found not only within the Roman Catholic Church. The book deals extensively with the experience gained through the evolution of the 'Bovendonk' approach to priestly formation, which later was broadened out to include permanent deacons. It tells us also what conclusions for the future may be drawn from the way this approach to formation has worked up to now.

Critically important is what the Rector himself writes of his experience of working with candidates of mature age. All those who are concerned or interested will discover in his contribution something of the background thinking behind the distinctive policies which inform his approach: matters for which he assumes responsibility, but which will greatly help a fuller debate on future policy. Looking back on my own formation, I can only say I wish that there had been as much openness.

I hope that this book will awaken an increased interest in this approach to formation, make it better known, and contribute to it being given a wider use in providing for Church ministry.

+ Hubertus C.A. Ernst,

Retired Bishop of Breda, The Netherlands.

Late have I loved You

Late have I loved you,

O Beauty

ever ancient, ever new,

late have I loved you!

You were within me, but I was outside,

and it was there that I searched for you.

In my unloveliness I plunged into the lovely things which you created.

You were with me, but I was not with you.

Created things kept me from you;

yet if they had not been in you

they would have not been at all.

You called, you shouted,

and you broke through my deafness.

You flashed, you shone,

and you dispelled my blindness.

You breathed your fragrance on me;

I drew in breath and now I pant for you.

I have tasted you, now I hunger and thirst for more.

You touched me, and I burned for your peace.

St. Augustine,
Confessions, Book X: Chapter XXVII
Hippo, 401

(http://feastofsaints.com/ancientnew.htm)

INDEX

    Foreword   5
        H. Ernst, bishop, The Netherlands
1. General Introduction   10
        M. Ham, R.C. diocesan priest, The Netherlands, Brazil

    Part I   History

2. The origins of the Bovendonk formation of priests   22
    H. Ernst
3. Preparing the way   27
    M. Ham
4. Part-time priestly formation in the Anglican Church   40
    J. Worthen, priest in the Church of England, U.K.

    Part II   Vocation: a way to go

5. Introduction to part II   53
    M. Ham
6. It is God who calls   61
    M. Ham
7. Responding with increasing inner freedom   78
    M. Ham
8. Learning from experience   114
    M. Ham
9. Late vocation: a personal reflection   165
    H. van den Blink, priest in the Episcopal Church, U.S.A.

    Part III Evaluation

10. Bovendonk programme, an evaluation   189
    J. Snijders, Marist, The Netherlands
11. Bovendonk, another path to priesthood   200
    K. Rafferty, c.m., Ireland

1. GENERAL INTRODUCTION

By Matt Ham

A part-time programme of formation, designed for middle-age men in full-time employment, is not the most common or best known route to priesthood in the Roman Catholic Church. Still, it is more than just another option: it is recommended by the Church as a form of training that can and should be offered to mature men, alongside the other options of the seminary, or residency in a student community whilst attending university.

Another option

The *Code of Canon Law* (can. 233,§ 2) states that 'priests, and especially diocesan bishops, are to take care that men of more mature years who believe they are called to the sacred ministries are prudently assisted by word and in deed and are duly prepared'.

And in the Post-Synodal Apostolic Exhortation *Pastores Dabo Vobis* (PDV) number 64, Pope John Paul II writes 'We should also mention the phenomenon of priestly vocations arising among people of adult age after some years of experience of lay life and professional involvement. It is not always possible and often not even desirable to invite adults to follow the established theological curricula of a major seminary. Rather, after a careful discernment of the genuineness of such vocations, what needs to be provided is some kind of specific program to accompany them with formation in order to ensure, bearing in mind all the suitable adaptations, that such persons receive the spiritual and intellectual formation they require'.

All over the world, there are dioceses and religious orders which make a special effort to provide these so-called 'late vocations' with a process of formation tailored to their situation. Yet in practice this often means candidates simply follow a shortened programme of training, or may even be expected to adapt to 'classical' seminary patterns.

Not all that exceptional

For centuries prior to the Council of Trent (1545 – 1563), it had been common for men to become priests at a later stage in life; indeed, in one sense it may even have been the norm.[1] The custom of beginning priestly formation around the age of twelve really only became established after Trent. But one consequence of the French Revolution, and the subsequent laws forbidding the recruitment of new members into Religious Institutes, was the serious shortage of clergy that occurred in the first decades of the 19th century.

This prompted the foundation of a special formation programme for older seminarians 1820, at Besançon in France. By 1873, the Salesians had also set up a shortened version of the classical formation model for older candidates, though this later reverted to the regular seminary format. Much the same thing happened in other countries, where similar institutions were also founded.

Following this trend, a special religious congregation known as the Missionaries of the Holy Family was founded in the Netherlands at Grave for so-called 'late vocations'. By 1960, the Dutch Church had four such institutes for mature seminarians: the Nazareth College in Horst, the Franciscan Antonianum in Amsterdam, the Jesuit Schola Carolina in the Hague and the 'Latin School' in Gemert – although the last one was in fact a minor seminary for young men above the normal school age who were preparing to join the ordinary major seminary.[2] In 1960, the Latin School in Gemert, (founded in 1587 as one of the initiatives of the counterreformation) still had a hundred pupils; by 1969, it had closed.[3]

Already by 1958 it had been argued that it is potentially misleading to speak of 'late vocations': there are in fact two routes to the priesthood, the standard major seminary route, and the pathway for mature men, which should carefully reflect the distinctive needs of older candidates. In the Latin School at

---

[1] Dellepoort, J.J., *De Priesterroepingen in Nederland. Proeve van een statistisch-sociografische analyse*, Den Haag, 1955, quoted in Stratum, J. van, in *Berna ut Lucerna: De abdij van Berne 1857-2007*, chapter 11: "Berne en de Latijnse School van Gemert", pag. 181-188.

[2] Idem, p. 181.

[3] Idem, p. 183.

Gemert, this basic principle had already been clearly established - witness the great freedom students had within that programme, compared with the more traditional approach found in residential minor seminaries.

At Bovendonk, however, as at Jumet and Antwerp, this principle was extended further to cover *all* the training, at major seminary level as well as the preliminary stages of formation. The net result is a process of formation which makes it possible for older candidates to build on their professional experience and study for the priesthood on a part-time basis, as they continue to exercise their secular profession.

Founding the institution and its predecessors

Msgr. Hubert Ernst, Bishop of Breda from 1967 to 1992, took the exhortation of Canon Law seriously (*Pastores Dabo Vobis* is of 1992), and with the support of his fellow bishops, set up a part-time course for priestly formation in Hoeven. The idea was not new: in 1968, a priest in the Diocese of Antwerp called Emiel Tobback had been asked by his bishop, Msgr. Daem, to establish 'a seminary for working men for the Flemish speaking part of Belgium'. This *Centre for Priestly Formation for Men of Mature age* started officially on 4th January 1970 as an inter-diocesan institute, and continued until August 1999. During those 29 years, 98 students completed the course and were ordained as priests. But even that initiative was not the first: the bishops of the French speaking dioceses of Belgium had already appointed another priest, Ernest Michel, to found 'a seminary for workers'.

As a consequence, the *Séminaire Interdiocésain Cardinal Cardijn* was founded in a former vicarage with a Rector in Jumet. Falling numbers of students forced the closure of the Centre in 1990, and the closure of the Dutch-speaking seminary followed at a later stage for the same reason – sadly, a trend in Belgium as well as the Netherlands, although in the Netherlands maybe a little less strong. Even at that time, declining numbers of vocations to the priesthood had a serious impact on all forms of training of all age groups, and this is a problem which persists up to the present day.

At the same time, concern over changing patterns of ministry was driving a similar agenda across the English Channel. In 1960, a part-time programme priestly formation had been pioneered in the Diocese of Southwark in the Church of England. From this initial experiment, a number of other part-time programmes subsequently developed across Anglican dioceses. There are currently eleven regional Courses training men and women for the priesthood, together with a number of smaller diocesan programmes for older candidates known as Ordained Local Ministry Schemes (OLMs).

The combination of these part-time programmes means that more ordinands in the Church of England are now trained in such courses than in the established full-time residential Colleges. Interestingly, the initial Anglican experiment was much influenced by continental debates about the need to improve access to ordained ministry for mature candidates; although, as Jeremy Worthen elaborates in the article that is included in this collection, the full extent of this reciprocal influence across the Channel is not entirely clear.

Formation of deacons

Msgr Ernst recalls that during the discussions that led to the establishment of the Bovendonk project the idea of extending the provision to include the training of permanent deacons had already been raised. When Msgr. van Luyn, Bishop of Rotterdam, therefore, asked Bovendonk in 2001 to accept candidates for the diaconate, his request was quickly answered. Thus *Priesteropleiding Bovendonk* (POB) became *Priester- en Diakenopleiding Bovendonk* (PDOB), training both priests and deacons.

Candidates for both ministries follow much the same basic curriculum over a six year period, with specific courses and formative elements inserted for each distinctive group. The length of the programme for diaconal candidates far exceeds the training required canonically, as well as the normal period of preparation on other courses. At this point in time, only three deacons have completed the programme and have now been ordained.

There are other part-time programs for deacons in the Netherlands. But the programme at Bovendonk is unique. Although the primary focus in Part II of this book is on priestly formation, important aspects of diaconal formation are also briefly considered, as is the way the two ministries mutually influence each other. The discussion is necessarily incomplete, because the diaconal programme is still developing, particularly in relation to the needs of married candidates. Furthermore, there is little other experience as yet with which to compare the situation at Bovendonk. As far as I know, there are no other formation programmes where candidates for the diaconate and priesthood work alongside each other.

General formation plan

As already mentioned, Canon Law and *Pastores Dabo Vobis* recommend a process of priestly formation specifically designed for older candidates. But within this general framework, bishops or major superiors are expected to use their own judgement in developing suitable training programmes. Thus, one might develop an apprenticeship model, where the candidate is placed in a parish to work for a few months under supervision of an experienced priest; another might develop a complete three year, full-time or part-time curriculum within a residential framework; and yet another option might be to devise a schedule of courses to complement earlier theological studies or using a course built round part-time study – or perhaps even a mixture of the two (what is known in the Anglican world as 'mixed mode training').

The programme at Bovendonk aims at 'forming professionally qualified men for the priesthood or the permanent diaconate in such a way that, with their background in secular life, they will be able, spiritually, pastorally and theologically, to start their priestly or diaconal ministry in a responsible way within the context of a parochial or regional team'.

The Foundation Constitution for the Bovendonk Institute puts it this way: 'The Institute will offer men who, after a professional training, hold or held a secular job, and who are actively involved in their parishes, a specific training pathway for pastoral work as a priest or a permanent deacon in the Roman Catholic Church. Theological, spiritual and pastoral aspects of formation will form a coherent whole, and integrated with their own experience in life and profession. Thus, candidates will pass through this process of formation, not individually, but as a group'.

Bovendonk admits Dutch-speaking candidates who have been formally sponsored either by a diocese or by a religious institute which supports the work of the Institute. Candidates must be aged 28 years or over, though in the case of candidates for priestly formation, students should not be older than 48 – although in practice there have already been some exceptions made to this rule.

Candidates must be able to meet the necessary academic standards - normally those required for entry to higher professional training. They should be professionally qualified, in current employment, and able to support themselves financially. During the six years of training, candidates follow an intensive programme of study, attending 20 or 21 weekends at Bovendonk each year, lasting from after work on Friday evening through Sunday afternoon. The curriculum is structured around the daily Eucharist, Holy Office and other times of prayer, and includes seminars and lectures, personal and group counselling, conversations to help integrate the student's experience, as well as time for recreation.

The entire programme is based on the four pillars of personal, spiritual, intellectual and pastoral formation. Specific goals and criteria for assessment are set for each of these core areas. During the first four years of training, students keep their secular jobs, and study part-time. After four years, however, students give up their secular employment and move into a full-time parish placement supervised by the Institute. This enables candidates in the last two years of training to spend more time working with the faculty at Bovendonk, processing their developing pastoral experience under supervision, engaging in theological reflection, and focusing directly on their own ministerial formation.

The Institute at Bovendonk is governed and guided by a Board of Management working under the jurisdiction of the Bishop of Breda. There also is a Consultative Body, made up of representatives from each of the dioceses and religious orders with students at Bovendonk. The core faculty is made up of the Rector, the Director of Studies, a priest responsible for supervising Pastoral Studies and placements, a permanent deacon responsible for supervising the diaconal candidates, and a Spiritual Director.

Adjunct lecturers consists of men, lay and ordained, and women who teach specific modules or offer personal direction and counselling. Several of the team have been associated with Bovendonk for many years. Mentors and supervisors are, whenever possible, women who are not only knowledgeable in the human sciences but experienced in spirituality as lived faith.

Most of the cost of training is borne either by the diocese or the religious institutes or orders that send candidates to Bovendonk. The ordinary also nominates a representative to take pastoral responsibility for the candidates, and in some cases, students may be required to undertake additional training locally in preparation either for incardination or for their future role in their particular religious community. They may also need to acquire other priestly or pastoral skills required for the work they will undertake after ordination in their place of work.

All of this requires close cooperation between Bovendonk and the candidate's diocese or religious order. This shared responsibility is powerfully symbolised at the moment of ordination, as candidates for the priesthood are ordained deacon in Bovendonk, but priested in their own diocese. In the case of deacons, however, the closer relationship with the Bishop embedded in the role of the Permanent Deacon is symbolized as faculty from Bovendonk present the candidates for ordination in their own diocese.

Tried and tested

From the foundation of Bovendonk in 1983 up to the present time (Summer 2007), 78 priests and 3 permanent deacons have been ordained after completing the Bovendonk programme of formation. These candidates have come from one Belgian and six Dutch dioceses, and eleven religious orders. 57% of the candidates starting the programme have been ordained. The average age at ordination was 43. One former student later left the priesthood; to date, no former student has been involved in any case of scandal or abuse. Of the vast majority of students it can be said 'they did well'.

This clearly demonstrates that this model of formation compares at least as well, if not better, to other more established systems preparing priests and deacons for parochial ministry. When the

Bovendonk programme was first launched in 1983 there were doubts but after 24 years we can safely say the model has proved itself. Judging from these results, the time is ripe to publicise this model more widely. The present English translation is based on the Dutch publication. The Dutch and English versions will hopefully, in due course, be followed by a Brazilian Portuguese translation. It may be that the Bovendonk model will attract international interest and encourage people in other countries to take similar initiatives.

This book and its authors

There are three parts to this book. Part One looks at the history of Bovendonk. The first article is from the hand of Bishop H. Ernst (1917), Emeritus Bishop of Breda, and founder of the Institute. Msgr. Ernst made a careful study of all the options before deciding to take this initiative. He also joined the faculty, lecturing on Moral Theology. Even today, he is indirectly but intensively involved with the Institute, keeping abreast of all the developments.

The Bishop's essay is followed by an interview with Emiel Tobback (1929), a priest from Antwerp, about the origin and development of the Walloon and Flemish antecedents to the Bovendonk venture - Emiel was the Director of the Flemish Institute for Priestly Formation for mature men for 26 years. The third article in this first section is a contribution by the Rev. Dr. Jeremy Worthen (1965) principal of the South East Institute for Theological Education in Kent, the second biggest centre for priestly formation in the Church of England.

Three of the four chapters in Part Two are written by me, M. Ham (1955). The first essay looks at the theme of vocation in sacred scripture and the second, based on material presented to First Year students, considers the human response to God's call. This is followed by a personal reflection on the experience of preparing older candidates for ordination, drawing on both my own background and my twelve years' experience as Rector of Bovendonk.

I try to explore some of the unique questions that this part-time has made me aware of. Every approach has its limitations but, after a general introduction, I have chosen in this essay to consider matters that have naturally demanded my attention as students work through the process from initial application and acceptance onto the course, through the six years of training, and onwards towards ordination.

I remain firmly convinced that a priest's pastoral effectiveness is directly related to his psycho-spiritual integration, and to his personal maturity, which form the basis of his intellectual and pastoral competence. I therefore approach the formative process mainly from the psycho-spiritual angle.

The fourth chapter of Part II draws on an address given by the Rev. Dr. Han van den Blink on the occasion of the twentieth anniversary of Bovendonk on 24 October 2003. Born into a Dutch Reformed family in Indonesia, Han (1934) is a pastoral theologian and psychotherapist. He immigrated to the United States from the Netherlands in his twenties, became a communicant of the Episcopal Church, and was on the faculty of Bexley Hall Seminary. He was ordained priest later in life. From his own experience, therefore, as a 'late vocation' Han reflects on the spiritual journey that candidates have to undertake, as he did, by exploring the true meaning of purification and *hesychia.*

Part Three contains contributions by two people who also speak from experience. The first is the philosopher Fr. Dr. Jan Snijders, S.M. (1928). Jan worked as a missionary in the Solomon Islands, and was subsequently General Secretary of the general administration of his Congregation in Rome. Throughout that period, he travelled widely and visited missionaries all over the world. Afterwards he taught philosophy at Holy Spirit Seminary, Bomana, in Papua New Guinea. Back in the Netherlands, he became Assistant Secretary to the Bishops' Conference, and Provincial of the Dutch Marist Fathers. He taught the first-year students at Bovendonk for fifteen years. In his paper, also given on 24 October 2003, Jan looks back over the twenty years of the Bovendonk project to assess its achievements, strengths and weaknesses and look ahead to the future.

Finally there is a report of the visit of Fr. Dr. Kevin Rafferty C.M. (1929) to Bovendonk in 2004. Fr. Rafferty is a philosopher, and was Provincial of the Congregation of the Vincentians in Ireland, as well as Director for many years of the inter-diocesan All Hallows College in Dublin. Since his retirement, he researches alternative models of formation for laity and clergy across

Western Europe, for possible use in Ireland. As a guest in Hoeven, we had long discussions about formation during which he did not hesitate to ask some penetrating questions. Later on we were also able to continue our exchanges in Dublin. His report is given here in an abridged form.

Acknowledgements

Finally, a few words of thanks. I think first of Margit Kaspers, who generously accepted my invitation to take a critical look at the Dutch text of the papers included in the original edition. Patricia Valkenburg, secretary of Bovendonk, was similarly always ready, in the smiling and efficient way that is typically hers, to rush to my aid and to push things along. I owe a great deal of thanks for the support given to me in so many different ways by my wise mentor, Fr. Jan Snijders, S.M., who took on most of the translating work, and my dear friends Alan Le Grys and Han van den Blink who accepted to revise Jan's' translations, enriching the English edition.

I thank Gerard de Rooij, Treasurer of the Diocese of Breda, and Bursar of the Institute, not only for finding the funds for the Dutch publication, but also for all his support over the years: 'you look after the formation', he used to say, 'so that we get good priests and deacons; I'll look after the money'. Nor will I forget Franck Ploum, who advised me in the final phase of putting the book together, and who also co-ordinated the Dutch publication with expertise and enthusiasm.

I thank the Lord who placed me at Bovendonk, where I have gained the experience that has had such a profound impact on my own understanding of formation. I thank Bishop Dr. Martinus Muskens who trusted me with this work, and his predecessor Bishop Hubertus Ernst who has always been so supportive, particularly in the early years, always ready to offer his insights and knowledge about the entire field of formation.

I thank the staff who loyally carried the burden with me, even during those times when I am sure I was not an easy colleague. I thank the lecturers and the supervisors who did much of the hard work, but also shared the task of thinking through the questions and issues of formation.

In the end, it was actually the conversations with students over the years that has helped me to understand the importance of this project. They convinced me of the value and validity of a dedicated part-time formation programme for older candidates. They may not have realized it at the time, but I came to appreciate profoundly their perseverance, spirit of sacrifice, and the trust they placed in me and my staff. To them and to all who have been, are, and will be connected with Bovendonk I dedicate this book.

Hoeven, 14 May 2007

PART I:

HISTORY

2. THE ORIGINS OF THE BOVENDONK FORMATION OF PRIESTS

By H.C.A. Ernst, former Bishop of Breda

Introduction

In the early 1980s, a suggestion was put forward to establish at Hoeven, on the site of the former major seminary of the diocese of Breda, an institute offering part-time training for the priestly formation of mature students - men who held regular jobs, but who felt called to move into ordained ministry. After the previous seminary closed, the buildings at Bovendonk had been turned into a Conference Centre. But Toon Hommel, a priest of the diocese of Breda who had founded the Center, and was its director, could see other possibilities: he proposed that the buildings should also be used for the training of priests and pastoral workers.

Filling a Gap

I was the Bishop of Breda at the time. My initial response to Fr. Hommel's proposal was that I felt there were already more than enough places for the people who wanted to undertake a course of training for lay pastoral work. We had various Catholic Institutes offering courses in theology at university level. Most of these had been founded in the1960s, when the major diocesan seminaries and those belonging to religious orders were closed.

There were also a number of other institutes, open to both men and women, offering pastoral training at a lower academic level. The assumption was that after these students had completed their training, they would combine pastoral work for the Church with their on-going secular employment.

Yet the idea of a dedicated training programme for men who wished to study for the priesthood while continuing their secular occupation was particularly appealing. Elsewhere, declining numbers of candidates were coming forward for full-time programmes of priestly formation. With the exception of the Ariëns House in Utrecht, attempts to open residential houses linked to the academic institutions had not been a great success.

Given this shortage of candidates, the idea of a specific scheme for men in secular employment appeared to fill an obvious gap. It would provide space for those who were still exploring the notion of priestly vocation, providing candidates with an opportunity to continue in their employment whilst working alongside others in a similar position.

So the core components of the programme started to emerge around the idea of combining philosophy and theology with pastoral training, within a framework of liturgy and prayer, in order to promote personal spiritual growth. These special arrangements would mean that careful attention could be given to the proper management of transition from secular life to ordained ministry, and all that this entails at a professional as well as a personal level.

Experiences

Earlier experiences confirmed my sense that this kind of program was well worth trying. I had taught Christian doctrine at an institute training social workers at a time when there had been a huge demand for social workers but few candidates. Somebody took the initiative to set up a part-time training scheme to enable people in other professions to negotiate the process of career-change. Set up as a temporary arrangement, it soon became permanent, as it became evident that older candidates with previous experience in other professions often produced social workers who were just as competent as younger people who had undertaken full-time training.

My predecessor as Bishop of Breda, Msgr. G. H. de Vet, had already established a training scheme for lay pastoral assistants. Reflecting the educational culture of the day, this program provided courses in philosophy, theology, pastoral praxis, and personal spirituality. Known as Maartenshof and led by Dr. Ad F. Vermeulen, O.S.A, the training was based in Breda, and open to both men and women. It had been a great success, and many graduates had shown that they were perfectly capable of working independently in the pastoral field.

Unfortunately, I was later forced to close Maartenshof because another diocese withdrew their students, and the Diocese of Breda was unable to continue the program by itself. The other diocese had initially support the Center but now felt that enough graduates were coming from other training programs that were established after ours had been set up. Still, the experience had enabled me to see another model of training in operation.

An Exercise in Collaboration

There was a precedent: the Flemish bishops in Belgium had already established a similar training program on an experimental basis. This was known as the Center for Priestly Formation for Men of Mature Age (CPRL), and had been established in Antwerp, under the direction of Emiel Tobback as Rector. Initially, I sought the advice of a diocesan commission, but their response was mixed, so I decided to go to Antwerp to see for myself.

My investigations convinced me that a programme of a similar kind in the Netherlands was not only possible and achievable, but also a positive way forward - although I could see that such a program would not be viable unless several dioceses agreed to participate. I therefore reported back to the Dutch bishops, and discussed the proposal with my colleague bishops who showed an interest.

The outcome of this conversation was that we agreed to set up a plan for the priestly formation of candidates in secular employment who wished to prepare for ordained ministry but could only train on a part-time basis. The plan already allowed for the possibility that at a later stage training for the diaconate might be included. It was agreed that the Bishop of Breda would carry episcopal responsibility for the program, though other dioceses or religious orders who wished to participate would be invited to become members of the Board of Advisors.

This structure was chosen because under Canon Law diocesan bishops are responsible for seminaries under their jurisdiction, but other bishops also need to retain pastoral oversight of their own candidates for the priesthood. The project had the full support of Cardinal J. Willebrands, Archbishop of Utrecht at that time. The archdiocese from the very beginning has actively supported the Bovendonk program.

Start of the Bovendonk Training Program

It was difficult to estimate how many candidates might come forward. In consultation with episcopal colleagues, therefore, it was decided to give the project some publicity, and then wait to see what would happen. We set a minimum requirement of five candidates for the plans to go ahead. In fact, we had twenty-six applications and this made it possible for the Bovendonk program to start on 23rd October, 1983 with the 17 students who had been accepted.

It was not difficult to find a Rector: Fr. Dr. Ad F. Vermeulen, OSA, was the obvious candidate. He had already demonstrated his competence as Rector of Maartenshof, the part-time course for pastoral assistants in Breda. Under his leadership, a formation curriculum was developed. We were able to obtain the services of highly committed lecturers, several of whom had previously taught in seminaries run either by dioceses or religious orders.

The plan was to adopt a two-stage structure for the course: for the first four years, candidates would work at academic studies and pastoral formation while continuing their secular employment. Then, they would give up their work and spend the final two years combining academic studies with a practical pastoral placement.

We were able to obtain the help of lecturers from the University of Tilburg and from various other university faculties of theology. Bovendonk has always been fortunate to have the support not only of committed students, but also equally committed lecturers, mentors and other helpers.

The Congregation for Sacred Education in Rome, which has overall supervision of seminaries, Catholic universities and faculties of theology, was informed of the establishment of the seminary at Bovendonk, and from that point on, the Priester Opleiding Bovendonk, as the seminary was officially known, has been regularly included in the cycle of Apostolic Visitations that are carried out by the Congregation.

The Formation of Permanent Deacons

At the request of the Bishop of Rotterdam, Msgr. A. H. van Luyn, S.D.B., the program at Bovendonk was enlarged in 2001 to include training for the permanent diaconate. The diocese of

Rotterdam had already collaborated with Bovendonk for a number of years. For the first four years diaconal candidates follow almost exactly the same curriculum as candidates for the priesthood. The last two years are designed to reflect the distinctive needs of diaconal ministry and the programme is centred on a pastoral placement directly related to this form of ministry.

The specific nature of this formation

We soon discovered that the transition from a secular occupation to ordained ministry has a far greater impact on the candidate's personal life than we had initially anticipated; rather more guidance and support was thus required than we had expected. So Bovendonk had to learn to adjust over the years, to provide for this increased level of supervision and support.

As a result of experiences such as these, Bovendonk has developed a unique program which is able to respond sensitively to the specific needs of men who undertake the formidable transition from secular work to sacred ministry. The renamed Priester en Diaken Opleiding Bovendonk (PDOB) provides a rich resource for the whole Church. To safeguard this training program and ensure its continued viability, I believe that dioceses would benefit from entrusting Bovendonk with its candidates for the priesthood and diaconate.

3. PREPARING THE WAY
THE *SÉMINAIRE INTERDIOCÉSAIN CARDINAL CARDIJN* IN JUMET AND THE CENTRE FOR PRIESTLY FORMATION OF MEN OF MATURE AGE (C.P.R.L.) IN ANTWERP.

By Matt Ham

This chapter is based mostly on material gleaned from conversations I had with Emiel Tobback on 13th September 2005 in Antwerp and 5th October 2005 in Hoeven. It was a privilege to have this opportunity to meet Tobback, and I wish to thank him for the time we spent together. Apart from these conversations, I was also able to use two unpublished articles written in 1975 and 1976 by staff members of 'Jumet'.

Bovendonk offers a programme of formation for priestly and diaconal ministry which is unusual, if not unique, within the Roman Catholic Church. Unlike other seminaries, candidates at Bovendonk continue in full-time employment during the first four years of part-time study, before moving into the final phase of training as full-time pastoral assistants. So far, little has been written about the history of this distinctive model of training. Yet long before Bovendonk opened in 1983, other people had already tried to find new ways for men in ordinary employment to prepare for ordained ministry, most notably in France and Belgium. Amongst these early experiments, the Centre for Priestly Formation for Men of Mature Age (CPRL) in Antwerp, founded by the Flemish bishops in 1969, proved to be the most influential in terms of preparing the ground for Bovendonk.

Schools for late vocations

There were three residential seminaries in Flanders during the 1960s providing training for late vocations. These institutions were run by the Society of the Divine Word (S.V.D.), the Franciscans (O.F.M.) and the Salesians (S.D.B.), and offered a four year programme of preliminary training for older candidates who had left school without any formal qualifications. Those who successfully completed the course then went on to a major seminary, usually within the diocese. But as standards in secondary education gradually improved, the number of candidates requiring this preliminary training declined, and by1969 the Franciscan and SVD schools had closed. The Salesian institute continued a few years longer, but by this time, needs were clearly changing. Mature candidates no longer needed basic preliminary education but required a more flexible framework that would allow them to train on a part-time basis alongside their existing work commitments.

The decision

In May 1968 the Flemish bishops decided to found a seminary for adult working men. They asked Msgr. Daem, then bishop of Antwerp, to find a suitable person to head up the new programme, and in October 1968 Msgr. Daem invited Fr. Emiel Tobback to take on this responsibility. Tobback accepted and since this was to be an interdiocesan asssignment, he was formally appointed a few days later by Cardinal Suenens, the Archbishop of Mechelen/Brussel.

Emiel Tobback came to this appointment as an experienced Spiritual Director, specialising in work with young people and with members of religious communities. He was born in Boom in 1929, and had been ordained priest in the archdiocese of Mechelen in 1953. After ordination, Tobback studied mathematics at the Catholic University in Leuven, and subsequently taught maths at the diocesan college in Mol. In addition to his work as a lecturer, Tobback took on the role of chaplain to the local Union of Women Students (VKSJ), and subsequently became the diocesan chaplain for this Union. He was also a member of the Commission set up to co-ordinate, guide and support religious communities through the difficult years following the Second Vatican Council. All of these wider responsibilities ensured that Emiel Tobback became widely known throughout the diocese by the time of his new appointment.

Priestly formation in Jumet

Tobback was a real pioneer. He used every opportunity to gather information, test options, and to talk with anyone interested. He had been given an open mandate – mostly because no one quite knew what to do. There was no building, no programme, no team - nothing. Emiel remembered the three points that Cardinal Suenens had made during their first conversation: give the candidates plenty of history so they can put things in perspective and take only men with a lot of 'common sense'. The third point he made had something to do with 'considering carefully the candidates background'. Emiel told me with a smile that he took this last point to be an assignment to focus on working class men.

When Tobback took up his appointment in January 1969, Cardinal Suenens told him that the French-speaking Walloon provinces in Belgium had already started a training programme for working men to become priests. So he went to Jumet, near Charleroi, to meet his Walloon counterpart Ernest Michel, a priest of the diocese of Tournai. Tobback heard a story from Michel about a meeting of chaplains of the Walloon Catholic Youth Workers which had taken place in 1966.

One of these chaplains had arrived late, and excused himself by saying he had been delayed by a conversation with a young factory worker who wanted to become a priest but did not know how to go about achieving this goal. This triggered a lively exchange of similar stories. The outcome was that almost everyone present agreed it was virtually impossible for young workers to become priests, simply because it meant losing an income and being placed in an unsustainable financial situation in order to learn Latin and do two years of philosophy before going on to do a further four years of intensive academic theology, all of which would ensure the loss of the very thing the Church needed - their knowledge, experience and understanding of working class culture.

As a result, the chaplains approached the bishops of the Walloon province, and Ernest Michel was eventually appointed to found a new *Seminary for Factory Workers*. A team was put together made up of Michel, a priest from the diocese of Liège, and a Salesian. The new *Séminaire Interdiocésain Cardinal Cardijn* was opened in 1967 in the old, large and spacious rectory at Jumet.

The course started with ten seminarians, living in two ordinary houses on a working class neighbourhood. All of the seminarians were former factory workers, and all but two of them had given up their jobs to study full-time for the priesthood. In addition to the weekday programme at Jumet, these seminarians attended classes on Saturdays at the *Institut Superieur de Culture Ouvrière (*I.S.C.O.) in Charleroi.

This institute was run by the Walloon Christian Workers' Organisation to provide working class people with the opportunity to continue their secondary education over a four year period to gain the entrance qualifications required for the university programme at Louvain-la-Neuve. The seminarians were required to achieve this qualification in two years, however, so the Charleroi sessions were supplemented with special courses taught at Jumet, alongside other lectures and seminars. The entire teaching programme was then organized around a common life of prayer and meals shared by faculty and students together.

Initially, traditional academic theology had formed the core of the programme, but after two years, five of the original students had withdrawn, and the members of the staff were left with the feeling that the system was not working as intended. The problem, they felt, was that the transition from working life to an intensive academic environment was too abrupt.

Two years after the start of the new seminary, the faculty made the decision to adjust the structure of the programme. First, the academic framework shifted from an intensive full-time course to a week-end system and was tailored to meet the needs of each individual student. Second, all the students were expected to live at home during the week and work in secular employment as they followed a part-time syllabus built around two years philosophy and four years theology.

Widening the objectives

This change set the pattern for an ongoing process of evolution based on experiential learning. The *Séminaire Cardinal Cardijn* was originally planned to train only priests, but it was soon providing training for lay people as well – working men and women who wished to serve the Church in some capacity. These men and women met in four or five groups spread over Brussels and other parts of French-speaking Belgium. This meant that the programme was now dispersed over a large geographical area, and so the classes had to be reorganised.

Jumet remained the focal point for the three priests, who formed the permanent staff team, but a local priest was attached to each group, and core staff also went out from Jumet to give lectures. All the groups were then brought together several times a year for a weekend of prayer, worship and spiritual reflection.

Tensions and closure of the seminary

Emiel Tobback remained in contact with Jumet throughout its existence, and was a permanent member of the support group which acted as a 'think-tank' for the institute. The members of the Jumet team were constantly on the look-out for new ways to improve and adapt the content and structure of the programme while maintaining good adult education standards. They were particularly concerned to find the most effective way to help people from a working class background to grow in understanding and Christian discipleship.

But this concern to be flexible and sensitive to other educational approaches started to generate friction between the staff and the bishops. The priority for the staff was the formation of worker-priests, whereas the bishops wanted adaptable clergy who could function just as well in traditional forms of ministry. Influenced by developments in France, the Walloon Socialist Unions had become more assertive than the equivalent unions in Flanders. Even so, Jument had no intention of returning to the 1960s, and operated with a different model of ministry. Instead of the radical clergy of the 60s who had received a regular seminary training and subsequently chose to live and work amongst the working classes, Jumet simply wanted to take working class culture seriously as a starting point for priestly formation.

There was a reason that the seminary had been named after Cardinal Cardijn who was known internationally as a tireless worker for the Christian Trade Unions. The 'see-judge-act' method Cardijn developed through his work with youth groups was widely used at Jumet. Cardijn also thought it was crucially important to work on building up the self-esteem of younger people, both as human beings and as Christians. His approach was undoubtedly a major factor in inspiring a number of working class candidates to consider ordination, despite their limited education, in order to serve their own community.

When the number of priest candidates at Jumet started to decline compared to the number of lay-students who applied, the Walloon bishops decided to close the seminary down.

Back to Flemish-speaking Belgium

Emiel Tobback was appointed Rector of the new Flemish seminary in late 1968, and he began the new year by getting to know the bishops and the rectors of the seminaries. He also sought out many people with experience in adult education. The next step was to form a group to whose job it was to devise the best way this seminary should be organized. The group was made up of one priest from each of the Flemish dioceses and a representative from the Christian Social Union for labourers, farmers and craftsmen.

This core working group became a think-tank which guided the seminary through the first six years of its existence, and continued to act in an advisory capacity for several years afterwards. The decisions and proposals they put together about the structure and content of the programme were submitted regularly to the Bishops' Conference, which then discussed and approved the plans. Plans for the new seminary were widely advertised through diocesan newsletters and parish bulletins. In September 1969 the seminary began work with a preparatory programme for the candidates who had applied for admission forward. The first formal courses began in January 1970.

Getting started: purpose, name, and accommodation

The Rector of the new Flemish seminary quickly learnt a few essential lessons from his visits to Jumet – in particular:

- Don't imitate full-time courses as taught in regular seminaries
- Don't remove students from their regular employment and their own culture
- Do let students live in their normal working class environment.

With these lessons in mind, Tobback started to look for colleagues who might help him. He found one in the person of the Novice Master of the Redemptorist Fathers - a deeply committed and religious man who soon became a valued and creative colleague. This new faculty member also joined the core working group.

Tobback then proposed a radical re-structuring of the basic seminary programme. As at Jumet, the course should revolve around a series of residential weekends. At the Flemish seminary, there were to be seven weekends each term (that is, 21 weekends per year) for the first four years, with each weekend running from Friday evening until Sunday afternoon. Tobback argued against the 'Jumet-idea' that students should live outside the seminary in small communities and suggested instead that students should continue to live in their existing environment and accommodation. The core working group readily agreed with him.

In order to avoid unnecessary confusion Tobback wanted to drop the phrase 'late vocations' because this nomenclature was too strongly associated with the older established model that required older candidates to move into a full-time residential context, to study Latin and other academic subjects in preparation for a classical seminary education.

By contrast, the new seminary was to offer a distinctive model of priestly formation built around the four years candidates spent living and working in their own social environment before ordination. So, instead of being known as a 'late vocation seminary', the new institute became known as the Centrum voor Priesteropleiding voor mannen op Rijpere Leeftijd (CPRL), or *Centre for the Priestly Formation of Mature Men*.

The question of where to house the seminary was easily answered. The new diocese of Antwerp had been formed in 1962 and since it was considered normal at that time for each diocese to have its own seminary, building one had already begun by the time proposals for the CPRL were put together.[4] The new seminary was being built at the Groenenborgerlaan in Antwerp, made up of four separate blocks, each with three floors

---

[4] In 2006 four Flemish dioceses, i.e., Mechelen-Brussel, Gent, Antwerpen and Hasselt, brought their regular priestly training together in Louvain, in the John XXIII Seminary. Antwerp sends its older students to Bovendonk, where one has been ordained and three others are still studying (2007).

consisting of ten bedrooms linked to a communal kitchen and living room. The idea was to avoid the image of the classical seminary and have the students live and work in small groups instead.

The sisters supervising the maintenance and administration of the building were housed in an adjacent block, where there was also a large kitchen and dining hall, as well as accommodation for the resident staff. There was also a library, and another block housing the lecture theatres and teaching spaces, as well as a separate chapel. The new CPRL moved into one of the student blocks while construction was still going on, and at its peak (1984-1985) occupied half of a second block to accommodate the 47 students then in training.

The declining numbers of 'traditional' students for which the diocesan seminary had originally been intended meant that the full-time seminary never occupied more than a fraction of the complex. From the outset, the buildings were used by other organisations, including the Theological and Pastoral Centre of the diocese of Antwerpen (TPC).

Since this entire enterprise was financed by the national Bishops Conference, the presence of CPRL ensured that the entire operation took on an interdiocesan dimension. At the end of each year of study reports about general developments were made to the Bishops Conference in addition to CPRL reports on more specific matters relating to the seminary curriculum and staffing.

General Structure of the Training Program

Pre-admission courses

Before starting the six-year pre-ordination programme, prospective students had to take part in a preparatory year that was organised around ten Saturday afternoon sessions. The purpose of these classes was to enable applicants to gain a better understanding of the nature of priestly vocation but they also enabled staff to observe the students and assess their suitability for ordination.

At first, this preliminary assessment included psychological screening, though this was discontinued after a while because the psychologists refused to pass on confidential information they had obtained from their 'clients'. Tobback used these initial sessions to gather material for reports on each of the candidates, and these reports were submitted to the appropriate bishop for a decision about whether that person should enter into training.

Three stages

The programme itself was designed in three phases; stage one was dedicated to philosophy, stage two to theology, and stage three consisted of a pastoral placement which included further theological formation. During the first two stages, students spent the weekends, from Friday evening to Sunday afternoon, in residence at the T.P.C., where each student had a room of their own. Apart from these weekends, however, students continued to live in their own homes, kept up their existing employment, and, as much as the programme allowed, maintained their own social life.

At the end of stage two, (that is after four years), students gave up their work to enter into full-time preparation for ministry. At this point, the weekends started a day earlier, with Thursdays and Fridays given over to theological study. Outside these extended weekends, students in stage three lived in a parish, usually but not necessarily in their own diocese, where they engaged in practical pastoral work with the permission of their own bishop. At the end of each year of training, the Rector wrote a report on each seminarian, and presented this report personally to the student's bishop.

Completing the course and ordination

As each student moved towards ordination, Tobback would visit the appropriate bishop and give a verbal report on the candidate's progress in addition to the written *testimonium*. The final decision lay with the bishop. Candidates were ordained as transitional deacons one year after starting the pastoral placement, usually at the C.P.R.L. Ordination to the priesthood normally followed after the candidate completed the programme, usually in the original parish from which the candidate came, although ordinations for the diocese of Ghent were always in the Cathedral of that diocese. The Rector of the C.P.R.L. attended all the ordinations and presented the candidates to the bishop.

Tutorial support and level of study

The academic level of the courses, the lecturing methods used, and the personal support system for students were always carefully adjusted to reflect the fact that the candidates were working men. The work was tailored to take account of their age, experience, and the fact that they had an established track record as active Christians in a professional environment. They were used to earning a living and organising their own lives. They were mostly self-reliant people who were used to handling practical situations and to solving day-to-day problems. This meant that the Rector, lecturers, and all the other people involved in the programme, needed to recognise and respect the students as equals.

Throughout each phase of training, every cohort of students had its own group leader. It proved difficult to find diocesan priests to take on this role but, fortunately, there were priests from religious orders who were able to help in this way. The group leader attended as many of the events as possible, including lectures. He taught courses in spirituality himself and he offered pastoral care and support. He also led worship. He was a point of reference for the students. He lived among the seminarians, was available to answer their questions, listened to their problems, and encouraged them to take initiative and to move forward. In many cases he acted as a mentor but he was not their personal Spiritual Director.

The seminary programme insured that during the six years of study each candidate had the opportunity to work with three different group leaders. Care was taken to ensure that teachers were rotated during each phase to cover the course content.

Adjunct teachers were invited to contribute special classes in various theological disciplines. Most of these lecturers became closely attached to the institute. The level of teaching was keyed to existing requirements of graduate level education of Institutes in Belgium. Senior and adjunct faculty shared responsibility with core staff for the content of their teaching, the methods used, and assessment of the students.

According to Tobback, the theological content of the courses was moderately progressive. Examinations were mainly conducted orally. If Bishops had any reservations they were invariably focused on the liturgy. It happened, for instance that unauthorised Eucharistic Prayers were sometimes used. Following a conversation about this with several Bishops, the Rector promised to remedy the situation - which he did.

The seminarians could choose their own Spiritual Director from a list of priests or suitable laypeople who were known to them. They also chose one of the core staff to supervise their pastoral placement, while the priest in charge of the parish, or some other designated person, retained the responsibility for the practical day-to-day learning process of the student.

One of the lecturers was a psychologist and psychotherapist. If problems arose that the Spiritual Director or other staff could not handle, the student concerned was referred to this psychologist. Yet despite all these forms of support, Tobback admitted that mistakes were made. Men were recommended for holy orders who should never have been ordained. 'But', he said somewhat ruefully, 'is it really possible to avoid this?'

A few facts and figures

Seventeen candidates began the first preparatory year in 1969. Twelve of these subsequently progressed to the first formal year of study. Tobback estimated that around 50% of all students admitted over the years withdrew. Even so, when the seminary closed in August 1999, 98 priests had been ordained, mostly for the five Flemish dioceses, although a few belonged to religious orders and two candidates came from Dutch dioceses. By September 2005, one had left the priesthood.

Differences with Bovendonk

Despite the similarities, there are a number of important differences between the C.P.R.L. and its 'daughter' Bovendonk:

1. The C.P.R.L. had been built around an interdiocesan structure, whereas Bovendonk was founded by the bishop of the diocese of Breda who remains the sole canonical head to the present day. The difference is that under interdiocesan rules the Bishops' Conference is the overall governing body and appoints one of its

members to manage the seminary, whereas in case of a single diocese, the Ordinary has final responsibility.

2. Unlike students at Bovendonk, seminarians at the C.P.R.L. retained no formal contact with their home diocese during the period of training. Candidates were not usually interviewed by the bishop's officers responsible for priestly formation before they were accepted, and selection procedures were exclusively in the hands of the C.P.R.L. This meant that in practice a candidate was only seen by his Bishop towards the end of a six year period of training. This led to friction at times – the bishop's officers in the home diocese often felt excluded. By contrast, students at Bovendonk come into training only after they have been endorsed by their diocese or religious institute, and are thus known in the diocese right from the start.

The diocese itself retains responsibility for the student, and only delegates the task of formation to Bovendonk, often alongside an additional diocesan programme that students have to follow throughout their time in training. The episcopal delegate responsible for the priestly formation of each diocese has oversight of the student at all times. He is also the person who, after consulting with the Rector of Bovendonk, conveys the definitive recommendation to the responsible bishop as to whether or not the candidate should be ordained.

3. This structural difference is reflected in different arrangements at the C.P.R.L. and Bovendonk for such things as the annual retreat and personal supervision. In Antwerp these were the responsibility of the C.P.R.L., whereas at Bovendonk such matters remain the responsibility of the diocesan Rector or episcopal delegate.

4. Bovendonk keeps the basic three-staged structure developed at C.P.R.L, but arranged around a different pattern of learning and without the special year group mentors. At Bovendonk, first year students follow a special introductory programme, which is followed by a rotating lesson programme taught over three years to students in the second, third and fourth years. Fifth and sixth year students come together for the final phase of training, also built around a rolling programme, although at one stage, when numbers were considerably higher, each class met in separate year groups.

Initially Bovendonk also had an introductory year, but this was abolished some time ago. When applications started to go down, it proved more practical to admit students straight into the first year without the introductory programme. Bovendonk opted instead for a more intensive selection procedure. Prospective students were invited to sit in on residential weekends to get a feel for the program themselves. That also gave the staff an opportunity to get an impression of a candidate's suitability.

5. The final substantive difference of which I am aware is that students at the C.P.R.L. were given additional theology lectures on the extra study days during the final years of the pastoral placement while at Bovendonk these extra days are used to provide three hours of group supervision and three hours of group reflection on matters of pastoral theology. This is done in groups of three which remain together and work with the same supervisor and pastoral theologian during the entire two year period.

These differences illustrate the close relationship between C.P.R.L. and Bovendonk in the sense that both institutes shared a common philosophy built around the need to adapt the training to reflect the changing needs of both candidates and Church.

4. PRIESTLY FORMATION THROUGH PART-TIME STUDY IN THE CHURCH OF ENGLAND AND ITS RELATIONSHIP TO ROMAN CATHOLIC DEVELOPMENTS

By Jeremy Worthen

Introduction

In 1996, for the first time the total number of students preparing for ordained ministry in the Church of England through part-time forms of training exceeded the total number training at residential colleges. Although the figures have shown some variation in the subsequent decade, with overall numbers starting to rise in the late 1990s, falling off again after 2000 and then increasing once more in the past couple of years, the general trend towards formation through part-time study has continued and indeed accelerated in the past six years.[5]

Such formation happens in a variety of institutions, some of them regional "Courses" preparing men and women for both "stipendiary" and "non-stipendiary" (or "self-supporting") ordained ministries, others Diocesan "Schemes" focused on training for Ordained Local Ministry, a self-supporting ministry to be exercised within the ordinand's current church context.[6]

Clearly, factors such as the growth of non-stipendiary ordained ministry and the rising age profile of candidates generally have contributed to the increase in the provision of training through part-time study in the Church of England over recent decades. Nonetheless, it is clear that while the model of formation through part-time study may remain a rather perilously small and fragile plant in the Roman Catholic Church in northern Europe, in the Church of England it is both sizeable and well-established; in 2004-5 there were 636 ordinands training through regional "Courses," 169 training through diocesan "Schemes," and 501 training full-time through residential colleges.

---

[5] GS1574, paper presented at the July 2005 Synod of the Church of England.

[6] For an overview of ministry in the Church of England from a few years ago, see Gordon Kuhrt, ed., *Ministry Issues for the Church of England: Mapping the Trends* (London: Church House Publishing, 2001); a summary of forms of ordination training is given in chapter 17 by David Way, "Initial Ministerial Education."

The purpose of this short paper is to evaluate briefly the relationship between developments in the Roman Catholic Church and the history of training through part-time study in the Church of England. In terms of the origins of such training, it will be argued that, while there is no evidence of direct contact between the pioneering experiments in priestly formation through part-time study that emerged at roughly the same period in the Church of England and in the Roman Catholic Church in north-west Europe in the 1960s, there were common motivations and shared concerns about the adequacy of inherited models of priesthood and training. These concerns had been most sharply articulated in the post-war period in Roman Catholic France and they found particular expression in the worker-priest movement there.

Moreover, personal contacts between Mervyn Stockwood, the key figure in establishing training through part-time study in the Church of England, and Roman Catholics may have had particular significance in shaping its earliest phase. In terms of subsequent history, the conscious fostering of contact between Anglican and Roman Catholic institutions across the divides of the Channel and of denominational difference over the past two decades will be noted prior to some concluding observations on how our common roots still keep us close to one another.

Worker-Priests, Priest-Workers and the Southwark Ordination Course

Priestly formation through part-time study began in the Church of England in 1960, with the founding of the Southwark Ordination Course (originally the Southwark Ordination Training Scheme) by the recently appointed Bishop of Southwark, Mervyn Stockwood. This was one of Stockwood's first initiatives, flagged up already in his enthronement address in 1959, and as a major institutional innovation it is inextricably bound up with Stockwood's pioneering ministry.

It is interesting to note that in the same year as Stockwood became Bishop of Southwark, his immediate episcopal neighbour, the Bishop of Rochester, had opened his own diocesan training centre for clergy, located within the precincts of the Cathedral, with the express hope that the Cathedral Chapter would be "fathers-in-God of ordinands... with a little group of retired clergy to stimulate faithfulness."[7]

It would be hard to imagine a conception more antithetical to Stockwood's vision. He had already been involved in preceding decades with a number of key committees reviewing issues relating to ordained ministry in the Church of England, including one that had recommended a significant relaxation of Canon Law restrictions on clergy engaging in "secular" occupations. The committee, which reported in 1955, had justified its recommendations on missionary as well as pragmatic grounds.

Although there was lack of consensus on some of its proposals, Canon Law was amended in 1959 to give bishops the discretion to exempt priests from the usual limitations on employment.[8] With this (grudging) room for manoeuvre in place, Stockwood – now a bishop – was clearly keen to exploit it. To do so, he wanted to set up a new pattern of training through part-time study, one that would allow candidates for the priesthood to continue in their employment at least for the duration of their training if not beyond.

In Stockwood's eyes, the urgent missionary situation of the Church meant that removing those candidates from the normal flow of life to a Cathedral precinct and the care of a Cathedral Chapter and some retired clergy would have been the last thing needed. Instead, it meant taking risks, as Stockwood told his first Diocesan Conference, "in order that we shall do something to get alongside that large section of our society which has little or nothing to do with the Church."[9] Therefore Stockwood decided to press ahead with the introduction of a new and unprecedented approach to training – formation through part-time study – via what became the Southwark Ordination Course (quickly abbreviated as "SOC").

Of course, the new Bishop of Southwark needed other people to turn the vision into reality, especially given the pace at which he

---

[7] "Rochester's New Theological College is Blessed," *Church Times* 23/10/1959.

[8] Patrick H. Vaughan, "Historical Background," in Mark Hodge, *Non-Stipendiary Ministry in the Church of England* (London: Church House Publishing, 1983), pp. 9-17.

[9] Quoted in Eric James, *A Life of Bishop John Robinson: Scholar, Pastor, Prophet* (London: Collins, 1987), p. 76.

intended to proceed; another of his first acts as Bishop was to invite John Robinson, already a noted New Testament scholar and later to achieve fame as the author of *Honest to God*, to become his suffragan bishop, with a brief to oversee the introduction of the new training scheme.

Remarkably, the course structure that Robinson designed in a matter of months for the Southwark Ordination Course in 1960 – mid-week classes to take place in the evenings after working hours, regular residential weekends, an extended residential school and various placements and practical activities, with some element of University accreditation as well as validation by the Church of England nationally – remains the blue-print for the regional "Courses" in the Church of England to this day, even if the time commitments have been somewhat reduced.[10]

Perhaps the one place in the wider Anglican Communion to which Robinson could have turned for inspiration was the Episcopal Church of the United States of America, where the Diocese of Michigan, for instance, had established a "School of Theology" in 1954 "for lay visitors, lay readers, non-stipendiary clergy and perpetual deacons."[11] Robinson returned from a lecturing and preaching tour the USA in 1961 full of enthusiasm for the initiatives in lay and clergy education that he had encountered, but by then he had already established the essential outlines of SOC's curriculum and mode of operation.[12]

The new course immediately attracted far more students than it could accommodate; in 1961, Robinson reported 90 applications for the first year, with the maximum possible number of 30 men starting training in September 1960, as well as enquiries from three other dioceses interested in developing similar patterns of training.[13] All subsequent initiatives in part-time formation in the Church of England started from the basic model SOC had created at its inception in 1960, although of course they also acquired their own distinctive features.

---

[10] James, *Bishop John Robinson*, pp. 76-77. Copies of early versions of the SOC prospectus are held in the SEITE Archive in Chatham.

[11] http://whitakerschool.org/id2.html, consulted 3/11/06.

[12] "Letter from the Bishop of Woolwich," *Southwark Diocesan Leaflet* 113 (September 1961).

[13] "Letter from the Bishop of Woolwich," *Southwark Diocesan Leaflet* 113 (May 1961).

In the 1990s, however, a general review of training advocated a regional rather than diocesan framework for formation through part-time study. SOC ceased to exist in 1994, when the South East Institute for Theological Education (SEITE) took over its work, with not only the Anglican Dioceses of Rochester and Canterbury but also the Methodist Church and the United Reformed Church included alongside the Diocese of Southwark as equal partners in a common enterprise.

To what extent, then, did the origin of formation through part-time study in the Church of England owe anything to Roman Catholic developments? In terms of direct influence on institutional form and curriculum planning, the answer would seem to be entirely negative. Yet it terms of the wider set of concerns motivating people such as Stockwood and Robinson, the context of events in Continental Roman Catholicism is clearly of great importance.

They would have been well aware of the worker-priest movement in France following the end of World War II. Stockwood became one of the very few Church of England Bishops to give active support and encouragement to the small number of Anglican clergy who sought to live out a vocation as worker-priests in the post-war decades, in conscious parallel with the French pioneers and sometimes in active dialogue with English Roman Catholic counterparts.[14] Moreover, as already noted, Stockwood had been involved in a committee on Canon Law that submitted its report in 1955, just after the effective suppression of the worker-priests in France.

The report clearly reflected the concerns of the worker-priest movement in, for instance, its insistence that priests were not simply to be given freedom to engage in other forms of employment in order to augment the ranks of the clergy with unpaid and inevitably subordinate staff; rather, the report's writers said, it was "essential that the character and function of these alternative ministries should be thought out, at the outset, without reference to the extent to which they can supplement the work of the parish priest," even suggesting that such men "should be directly responsible to the bishop" rather than to the parochial clergy.[15]

---

[14] John Mantle, *Britain's First Worker-Priests: Radical Ministry in a Post-War Setting* (London: SCM, 2000).

[15] Vaughan, "Historical Background," pp. 14-15.

Perhaps unsurprisingly, this proposal was not adopted by Convocation, and indeed in subsequent history it has been easy for the institutions Stockwood pioneered with SOC to end up serving to produce just the kind of unpaid, assistant parish ministry that he did not regard as an adequate response to the real and urgent task facing the Church.

As already noted, Stockwood justified the "risk" he was taking in launching a new model of training by appealing to precisely the same diagnosis that had fired worker-priests like Henri Perrin: great sections of modern society were not so much hostile as simply indifferent to the life of the Church and the claims of the gospel, and there was now a daunting cultural gap to be bridged by the Church's mission in secularised Western societies as surely as there was in the "non-Christian" countries that had historically been the exclusive focus of missionary concern.[16]

Indeed, what has become the ubiquitous language of "non-stipendiary" ministry in the Church of England initially had no place in the vocabulary of the founders of SOC: candidates who proceeded to ordained ministry whilst remaining in secular employment were initially referred to as worker-priests and then subsequently as "priest-workers" (or, when being more specific, "priest-baker" etc.).[17]

The direct allusion, and implied comparison, with worker-priests in the Roman Catholic Church cannot have been lost on well-informed people. In setting out his plans for the new training initiative in more detail to the Diocesan Conference in 1960, Stockwood gave three reasons for supporting it. The first was to encourage older men with family commitments to consider training for ordination, clearly not a shared concern with Roman Catholicism. The second two reasons, however, relate directly to the burning issues of the worker-priest movement.

For Stockwood proceeded to say that training through part-time study was also designed to encourage younger men to be ordained who were at present deterred by the prospect of becoming detached from the society they wanted to serve

---

[16] Cf. Henri Perrin, *Priest and Worker: The Autobiography of Henri Perrin*, trans. and introduction by Bernard Wall (London: Macmillan, 1965).

[17] See the discussion of Mantle, in *Britain's First Worker-Priests*, pp. 228-240, who stresses how difficult it proved to sustain such an emphasis.

through entering the priesthood, beginning with immersion in the ecclesiastical micro-world of the residential college. He believed that formation through part-time study could promote the creative interaction between theological study and contemporary culture:

It is easy for theology to become departmentalised and for students to live in an ivory tower; it should not be so easy for the man who returns each day from his theological studies to his factory or office, as it should compel him to relate his learning to his experiences.[18]

Interestingly, Stockwood allowed that this result might also be achieved through a mixture of such traditional training with limited periods at SOC – possibly recalling the experiments in France with seminarians working for a while in industry, subsequently forbidden in 1953, as well as some parallel initiatives in England, most notably in Sheffield during the 1950s.[19]

Finally, and perhaps most importantly, Stockwood argued that his new model of training was needed for the sake of the "unchurched masses," whom he located particularly in the industrial areas of his South-London diocese. He was aware that these areas appeared to be consistently resistant to well-meaning evangelistic initiatives. He wanted to develop a different kind of approach to mission in such contexts:

"I envisage, for instance, a parish church which will have on its staff not only parochial clergy, but priests who will be earning their livings at different levels in the area – professional, social and industrial – and, because of that, playing a prominent part in the life of the locality. If that happens it may be possible to create a vigorous Christian community."[20]

This vision, set out by a pioneering Anglican Bishop from the broadly Catholic wing of that Church, would seem to be directly derivative from the ideals of the worker-priest movement in the Roman Catholic Church. It was a key element in Stockwood's own motivation for developing formation through part-time study and in his attempts to motivate others to support it as well.

---

[18] Mervyn Stockwood, *Diocesan Conference Speech: June 13th 1960*, p. 2. The original text of Stockwood's speech is in the SEITE Archive in Chatham.

[19] See Wall's Introduction to Perrin, *Priest and Worker*, p. 9; Mantle, *Britain's First Worker-Priests*, pp. 85-86 and 154.

[20] Stockwood, *Diocesan Conference Speech*, p. 2.

In addition to this general background, there is also the matter of Stockwood's personal contacts with Roman Catholicism. In his autobiography, he tells the intriguing story of an unexpected private audience with Pope John XXIII in 1959, with Monsignor Cardinale, the Papal Nuncio in Brussels, acting as interpreter. Stockwood's passion for promoting Anglican-Roman Catholic relations and explicit hope for the reunion of the two Churches were far from fashionable at a time when there was still widespread suspicion of Roman Catholicism in the Church of England, and he was reprimanded for participating in the impromptu audience by the Archbishop of Canterbury.[21]

Stockwood was not, however, a man to be much deterred by the criticisms of others. Back in Italy again shortly after his enthronement, but before the inauguration of SOC, he met up with Cardinale, whom he discovered lived in an ordinary block of flats in Rome along with another priest, out of a concern to establish contact with the people there who lived lives entirely cut off from the Church. The two of them had started an informal group that met in a common area of the apartment block and celebrated Mass with them.

As Stockwood reports it, "I was fascinated by what Cardinale told me because I was keen to implement the plans I had suggested in my enthronement sermon with regard to auxiliary priests."[22] In this context, he also makes it clear that his own overriding motivation for taking this step related to the second and third reasons he gave in his speech to the Diocesan Conference quoted above – to bridge the cultural divide between the clergy and a society in large part alienated from the institutional church.

What is also remarkable, however, is that it was not only a case of Stockwood taking an interest in contemporary Roman Catholic developments and drawing inspiration from them. When he had a private audience with the Pope again in 1963, he relates that John XXIII "was particularly interested in the Southwark Ordination Scheme and asked me to let him have full details."[23]

---

[21] Mervyn Stockwood, *Chanctonbury Ring: An Autobiography* (London: Hodder, 1982), pp. 98-101.

[22] Stockwood, *Chanctonbury Ring*, p. 105.

[23] Stockwood, *Chanctonbury Ring*, p. 121-22.

The Pope would have had a very good knowledge of the worker-priest experiments in France from his time as Papal Nuncio to Paris from 1944-53. It is only possible to speculate as to what he might have done with the information Stockwood gave him and the extent to which it might have encouraged him to support comparable initiatives within the Roman Catholic Church had he lived longer.

Crossing the Channel

In the decades following the foundation of the Southwark Ordination Course, a number of parallel programmes for formation through part-time study were created in the Church of England, with sixteen in total in existence by 1983, most of these serving more than one Anglican diocese and sometimes Free Church partners as well.[24] As already noted, all were replaced in the 1990s by a national network of regional Courses.

Given its proximity to the Continent, perhaps it should not be surprising that an institution based in the south-east corner of England, the Canterbury School of Ministry (CSM), developed a strong relationship with French Roman Catholicism just across the Channel following its inauguration in 1977. A twinning relationship between the Anglican diocese of Canterbury and the Roman Catholic diocese of Arras had already been established, and CSM built on this, holding one of its residential weekends each year in Arras at the Diocesan Centre (the former seminary) from the 1980s on.

As well as teaching sessions, some of them given by Léon Hamain, the Vicar-General of the Diocese who helped to facilitate the link, there was contact for visiting CSM staff and students with a house for Roman Catholic priests in the Diocese who were still seeking to live out the worker-priest vision, and clearly this was an area of particular interest; John Mantle, on the CSM staff at the time and now Bishop of Brechin in Scotland, eventually published a detailed study of British Anglican priests who had continued the model pioneered by Perrin and others into the last few decades of the 20th century.[25]

---

[24] Hodge, *Non-Stipendiary Ministry in the Church of England* pp. 15-16.

[25] See Mantle's account of his encounter with the French worker-priests of Arras in *Britain's First Worker Priests*, p. xxii.

A key component of the visits to Arras also became an initiative known as ADAP ("Assemblie Dominicale en l'Absence du Prêtre") for large, rural deaneries, which enabled authorised lay people to provide communion from the reserved sacrament during Sunday worship; Canterbury diocese was interested in introducing a similar model at one stage. As with the early days of SOC, it was shared concerns about responding to a post-Christendom context, and in particular how there might be creative developments in patterns of ministry to support this, that provided the most significant common ground.[26]

Despite such enriching contacts, however, it would seem the part-time model of priestly formation in the Church of England developed for 30 years in almost complete indifference to the fact that there were significant parallels in Continental Roman Catholicism, as discussed elsewhere in this volume. This changed in a small way, however, from the early 1990s, when Martin Baddeley, the then Principal of SOC, having been made aware of the existence of seminaries using part-time approaches in northern Europe, decided to explore the potential for establishing relationships with them.

The outcome of this was an informal "twinning" arrangement between SOC and the seminary at Bovendonk in the Diocese of Breda. When SOC and CSM were both replaced by SEITE as the new "Course" for the south-east region of England, SEITE's Principal, Alan Le Grys, continued and developed the link that SOC had established. As an integral part of their accredited programme of training, SEITE students in their final year of preparation for ordained ministry travel to Bovendonk accompanied by staff and share a teaching weekend there with the Dutch seminarians.[27] Clearly, there are great, if hard to quantify, benefits for students and staff on both sides from the sharing of experiences, participation in common worship and consequent broadening of horizons that take place at these weekends.

---

[26] I would like to thank Alan Amos, former Principal of CSM, and Trevor Pitt, former Vice Principal, who have been most helpful in providing me with information about these developments. Trevor Pitt has continued the link with Arras via the North Eastern Ordination Course, of which he is now the Principal.

[27] I am very grateful to Alan Le Grys, former Principal of SEITE, for his help with understanding how SOC and subsequently SEITE came to be connected with Bovendonk.

In recent years, there have been attempts to span the linguistic and curricular divides further by running a teaching session in which all the students come together and reflect on a topic of shared interest. SEITE staff and students have become aware of the distinctive approach to formation that has been developed at Bovendonk under the guidance of the current Rector, Matt Ham, drawing on the body of research work carried out by members of the Gregorian University's Institute of Psychology, founded in 1971.

Personal, spiritual and ministerial formation has been more clearly identified as a priority in the Church of England's training over the past decade and it has been valuable for SEITE to learn about Roman Catholic developments in this area. In its latest curriculum, SEITE allocates specific teaching sessions to the relationship between theological anthropology, psychology and vocational growth in a way that reflects this engagement.

Underlying these important points of contact and mutual learning, however, remain the same common concerns that were identified in relation to the origins of SOC in 1960. The Church of England and the Roman Catholic Church in northern Europe still hold in living, if fast fading, memory a time when they enjoyed a cultural and political power vastly greater than they do today, and must face some hard questions about how they respond.

Should we return to the old ways of the Church, in the hope that the former glories will then return with them? Do we turn our backs on what Stockwood called "the unchurched masses" and provide a niche service for those who still value our particular brand of institutional religion? Or do we seek to sustain a vision of mission to the whole of the society in which we find ourselves, including those who are alienated and indifferent, and grapple with the profoundly problematic issues that necessarily follow from that commitment?

The model of part-time training on both sides of the Channel descends directly from the post-war visionaries, Roman Catholic and Anglican, who wanted to say "no" to the first two of these questions and "yes" to the third. They realised that their "yes" meant contemplating very different expressions of ordained ministry from those that had become customary, and that openness to changing expressions of ministry required freedom for innovative patterns of training.

Above all, it meant embracing continuing direct engagement with contemporary society through paid work during priestly formation not as a way of saving money but as a positive initiative for preparing for a "mission-shaped" ministry – a priesthood not turned in on itself and the perpetuation of an ossifying ecclesiastical culture, but turned out to offer, in solidarity with all God's people, the good news of the kingdom of God to the world loved everlastingly by God.

PART II:

VOCATION, A WAY TO GO

5. INTRODUCTION TO PART II

By Matt Ham

What are the issues?

Working with adult men from widely diverging levels of education, employed in variety of professions, who have seen a lot of life and have had many varied experiences, whose personalities have developed and who have already have formed their own ideas about God and the Church, and yet still want to become priests, is very different from working with young candidates who come straight from school.

We must therefore ask: what is distinctive about this approach to formation? What are the contextual factors which suggest a need for a different approach? What additional material should such candidates be given, and what are the potential problems? Some people may even wonder whether it is possible at all to articulate clearly how this approach differs from other forms of priestly formation. And is any of this actually that important?

These questions were often discussed among colleagues. In my conversations with students I have tried to discern what the main issues are. I will try to discuss what I have discovered in the second part of this book. Why? Because over the years I have become convinced of the value of 'late vocations'.

Part-time formation is the only practical option for many men like these. It simply is not realistic to ask them to live with younger men in the residential context of the classical seminary. Older candidates are entitled to an approach that is tailored to their personal needs and development. Most of the priests trained at Bovendonk would never have been ordained had it not been for our part-time programme.

The Netherlands is fortunate to have three different models of priestly formation: the classical seminary, the student community near a university and the part-time model[28]. All three of them are

---

[28] In The Netherlands, in 2007, the dioceses of Den Bosch, Haarlem and Roermond have a classical Major Seminary, the archdiocese of Utrecht has a residence for seminarians studying at the Faculty of Catholic Theology or following a special program, called the integrated priestly formation. Breda is

legitimate, valuable and complete forms of training. Precisely because we have three options of equal value, we can look for the best fit, taking into account the age of the candidate, his previous education, and his level of maturity. It is not appropriate that the options for a candidate for the priesthood should be limited to the preferred model used in his home diocese, irrespective of his personal circumstances.

When dealing with a candidate for ordination, the only responsible question to ask is which model gives this particular person the best chance of becoming a good priest, given his age, level of personal growth, and character. Flexibility is needed: part-time formation is not always appropriate for an older man in full-time employment, but the classical seminary is not always the most appropriate way forward for younger men either.

Some young people would clearly benefit from being on their own for a while and earning a living. Older men used to taking care of themselves on the other hand could equally benefit from living in community. Each of the three models has its own dynamics, its own way of shaping spirituality and personal growth.

People in charge of priestly formation, and, of course, bishops, will naturally be led by an internal image of the 'ideal' priest: what sort of men these priests should be, what they should know, what skills they should have, and so on. This sets the agenda: what should we be looking for, what should we offer such candidates, and what is reasonable to ask of them? Experience has taught the Church to expect certain things in terms of the classical seminary and the communal formation of university students, but little attention has yet been paid to what can be gained from part-time model of formation. This is where I would like to make a contribution based on my own experience – gained the hard way, as usual, through trial and error.

---

responsible for the part-time programme for 'late vocations', and also sends younger candidates to Utrecht; Rotterdam entrusts its candidates either to the Utrecht scheme or to the 'late vocation' program in Breda, although older candidates from this diocese spend their last two years in training living together in a diocesan formation centre. Groningen-Leeuwarden sends its candidates to different institutes according to perceived need. With the exception of Den Bosch en Roermond, therefore, all Dutch dioceses and the Belgian Diocese of Antwerp send their older candidates to the part-time programme in Breda, although candidates who already have existing qualifications in theology may be placed on a special training pathway by their diocese or religious institute.

What approach to take

Without wanting to suggest naively that people can be neatly divided into separate components, my preference is to approach a candidate from the psycho-spiritual perspective rather than from the viewpoint of intellectual ability or perceived pastoral skills. Why do I believe this? I know pastoral practice cannot be separated from pastoral skill, but I want to consider them for a moment as two different aspects of an inter-related process. When I say 'pastoral practice', I mean the practical outcome of pastoral activity - what a pastor *does*, rather than his personal attitude or pastoral concern, or even his pastoral competence.

To put it bluntly, any normal person can learn a set of skills, like learning tricks. Anyone can adopt a pattern of learned behaviour. Atheists can study theology and spirituality, but that does not make them a Christian. In our case, teaching a man the 'tricks of the trade' does not make that person a priest in the Roman Catholic Church. Pastoral sensitivity, that is, the ability to *inhabit* priesthood, comes from a life lived with spiritual faithfulness in response to a personal call from God. The Lord calls a person into a relationship which leads towards service amongst the people of God. This means walking a path that can only be understood and experienced from within the framework of the Rule of Faith, rooted in reflection on Holy Scripture and the living tradition of the Church.

This presupposes a degree of philosophical and theological insight, of course. But we must also recognize that even within this framework, unconscious emotional factors continue to shape the process of psycho-spiritual and intellectual growth. So it happens that some very gifted students are sometimes unable to progress, simply because they are held back by internal restraint. I sometimes compare this in my teaching to a hot air balloon. You can turn up the heat, but if you forget to release the restraining ropes, the balloon simply will not leave the ground. More courses, more training, more input, will make no difference, except, perhaps to cause some serious damage because of increasing frustration. Only when the major psycho-spiritual knots have been released can the ropes be loosened and is it possible for the balloon to take off.

These are some of the important factors that have determined my priorities, based on my own training and experience in spirituality and psychology. I realize my approach will not directly address all the dynamics at work in priestly formation, and I also realize that by adopting one particular approach there is always a risk that other equally important aspects of formation will be lost. But this is a risk I am prepared to take, as I try to focus on those elements which seem to me to be of particular importance in the specific case of older candidates.

I will not discuss the most obvious aspects which should be considered like admission criteria and the level and quality of existing qualifications, but I will discuss the (older) candidate's academic and professional track record. For example, does this person tend to complete programmes of study, or does he have a habit of dropping out before the course has finished. Did he change jobs frequently? Such patterns of behaviour offer important insight into that person's psychological profile.

Another obvious, crucial point of interest is the personal history of an applicant. For example, if a candidate lost a parent or some other significant person during childhood this could have a profound impact on their subsequent development and the way this person has coped with the process of bereavement will have my particular attention. Yet, what could be of far greater significance might be the *timing* of an older person's decision to test a priestly vocation. For example, did the candidate present himself only a short time after the bereavement, and if so, what is this saying about their psychological motivation?

Sexual orientation is another obvious issue. Younger candidates are still developing in terms of sexuality and emotional maturity, and such people usually need time to settle down before they make far-reaching decisions. Because chronological age is no guarantee of maturity, older candidates are not necessarily that much more mature, and may still be struggling with their sexuality. On the other hand, they may have come to know themselves better, and so might be better equipped to speak about such matters more easily. Thus, I will not discuss these obvious questions relating to older vocations but concentrate on the more specific issues of psychological interest.

Overview of the second part

This second part of the book has three chapters. The first is based on course materials prepared for the First Years students at Bovendonk under the title *Vocation as Process.* I use examples from Scripture to show that each time God calls a person, the narrative suggests a pattern that points towards a dynamic process with some identifiable common features. Vocation is more than 'I feel God calls me', or 'I have decided to become a priest'. The vocational dialogue always happens in a context of concrete social, political, religious and personal relationships, even if the candidate does not always recognise this reality. There are always other people involved in the person's call.

Priestly vocation is specifically located in the Church, and the person who thinks he is called cannot make an independent decision purely on the basis of his own opinion. In other words, ordination depends on other people as well. It can be a sobering experience for candidates (and others, sometimes) to realise that the Church has her own criteria for assessing priestly vocation. This external point of reference may mean that older men especially have to face some searching questions about their character, identity, life history, and established way of life. All of these can acquire a wonderful taken-for-granted quality, but it may not always be fully appreciated that they may also been questioned by those responsible for their formation.

This book will not discuss the official criteria for ordination, not because I am against discussing them but because we have to work with existing ecclesial framework which in the context of training need to be accepted as a given reality for those considering ordination. As we shall see later on, clarity is an important factor in formation.

In Chapter Two, I describe the theological anthropology which provides a theoretical framework for training and formation at a psycho-spiritual level. Anyone who knows the Institute of Psychology in Rome will immediately recognize the influence of the Institute in my thinking. The late Father Luigi Rulla S.J. and his colleagues, including some of my mentors like Bart Kiely S.J. and Franco Imoda S.J., have pioneered research into the factors that influence people entering or leaving religious communities or the priesthood.[29] These are not the only researchers who have worked in the field,[30] and the Institute in Rome does not claim to be the sole authority on the psychology of vocation, but their work has certainly helped me to understand myself more clearly and fully, and I know that their work has also been of great significance to many others involved in the work of priestly formation.

The *Magisterium* has made a powerful call to the Church to make more use of the human sciences in the discernment and development of priestly vocation, yet many in the Church responsible for formation remain unconvinced of the usefulness of psychology. Perhaps this is the legacy of the damage done by certain schools of thought in the 1960s and 70s.[31] Others reluctantly concede that psychology might be important, but only, perhaps, as a necessary evil to be employed whenever the Church is presented with problematic candidates. But then it is usually too late, for at that point the damage has already been done. For that reason it would make more sense to follow the

---

[29] Rulla, L.M., S.J., Ridick and Imoda, *Anthropology of the Christian Vocation: Vol I, Interdisciplinary Bases*, Gregorian University Press, Rome, 1986, and *Vol II, Existential Confirmation*, GUP, Rome, 1989; *Depth Psychology and Vocation: a psycho-social perspective*, Pontificia Università Gregoriana, Roma, 1990.

[30] See, in particular: Arcidiocesi di Modena – Nonantola, Seminario Arcivescovile Metropolitano, *Orientamenti Formativi per gli alunni del Seminario Maggiore*, Modena 1993; Schutz, K., *Seminaries, Theologates and the Future of Church Ministry*, The Liturgical Press, Collegeville, 1999; Gambino, V., *Dimensioni della Formazione Presbiterale*, Editrice Elle Di Ci, Torino, 1993; Maciel, M., *Integral Formation of Catholic Priests*, Alba House, NY, 1999; McGregor, B., et. al., *The Formation Journey of the Priest: Exploring Pastores Dabo Vobis*, The Columba Press, Dublin 1994; Seminario Arcivescovile di Milano, *La Formazione del Presbitero Diocesano*, Centro Ambrosiano, Milano, 1995; Unites States Conference of Catholic Bishops, *Program of Priestly Formation*, Washington D.C., 1993 (1st ed.), fifth ed. August 4th 2006
http://www.usccb.org/vocations/ProgramforPriestlyFormation.pdf

[31] In 1963, E. Berne presented his ideas on transactional analysis, and this theory was developed by T.A. Harris in his book *transactional analysis (I'm Okay, You're Okay* (Harper and Row 1963*)*. The basic assumption behind this theory is that human beings look for self-fulfillment and satisfaction through social connection, and this, arguably, stands in some tension with the essence of the Christian vocation. The influential theories of Eric Erikson (1963) also lack a clear or explicit theological anthropology. Erikson, like Carl Rogers, rejects the idea that a human being should strive to achieve externally related goals in life; rather they should work for *self*-fulfillment. Despite the fact that these ideas are far from helpful in shaping Christian values but simply reflect the prevailing secularist ideology, they have nevertheless been used frequently by those involved in the formation of priests and religious.

highest authorities in the Church and make proper use of the human sciences wherever appropriate, to support the challenging but rewarding task of formation.[32]

To understand the process of discernment more fully, Rulla and his colleagues see no problem in bringing the insights of the *Spiritual Exercises* of Saint Ignatius[33] into dialogue with the theoretical framework provided by the human sciences. Rulla was deeply convinced that God's grace precedes every form of human endeavour, and his theory of theocentric self-transcendence and its practical applications builds freely on an interdisciplinary study of philosophy, theology, spirituality, depth psychology and social psychology. The title of his main work, *Anthropology of the Christian Vocation*[34], speaks for itself.

Logically, this present chapter should probably be followed by another setting out the theoretical and practical framework informing the model of formation presented in the first two chapters, and perhaps also consider the didactic and educational implications of this approach. However, this theoretical rationale for the pedagogy used at Bovendonk has already been published in *The Bovendonk Study and Formation Guide*, an 80 page booklet given to all new students, so I have not repeated the material in this publication.

The third chapter therefore sets out a series of reflections on what we have learned over the years from the many candidates who have passed through the system from admission through to departure (which could be either because they completed the training or because they withdrew, or in some case because they were asked to withdraw). For the sake of clarity, these reflections concentrate on the beginning, middle and end of the training process, although I fully recognise the danger of over-simplifying the complexities of psychological development as well as the danger of playing down the common threads which might be running through the entire process.

---

[32] E.g. John Paul II, Post- Synodal Exhortation *Pastores Dabo Vobis*, 25 March 1992, Vatican City, 1992. European Vocations Congress, 5 – 10 May 1997. Final document: *New Vocations for a New Europe,* Libreria Editrice Vaticana, Vatican City 1998.

[33] Ignatius of Loyola, *Spiritual Exercises*, transl. Louis J. Puhl, Loyola University Press, 1968.

[34] See note 2 above.

The fourth chapter in this section consists of a lecture given by Han van den Blink at Bovendonk on 23 October 2003, in the course of which he describes his own journey towards ordination as an older candidate. This is an impressive account of one person's experience. Han explores the complex spiritual, personal and psychological factors that move a candidate to embark on what is usually a long and often demanding process.

The material in this second section is inescapably selective but I will try wherever possible to make the connections with the theoretical framework for priestly formation to which I am committed. I do not claim that the matters discussed in this section relate only to the needs of older candidates - many of the issues discussed are obviously just as relevant to the training of other candidates, regardless of their age or the way they are trained. Nevertheless, the primary focus remains throughout on the specific experience of Bovendonk, and on the distinctive perspective we have gained through the privilege of working with mature students.

6. IT IS GOD WHO CALLS: THE VOCATIONAL PROCESS IN THE LIGHT OF BIBLICAL SPIRITUALITY

By Matt Ham

> *Now to Him who by the power at work within us is able to do far more abundantly than all that we ask or think, to Him be glory in the church and in Christ Jesus to all generations, for ever and ever. Amen.* (Ef. 3, 20-21)

Deciding on a vocation

If it is not easy to speak about vocation, to decide upon one is even more difficult. When can you say that somebody has a vocation? When not? Who has or does not have a vocation? I do not see how anyone can possibly come to the conclusion that a particular candidate does or does not have a vocation on the basis of a few initial interviews. There are, of course, situations in which the ordinary criteria for admission are evidently missing. That does not mean the person will agree if he is turned down, and perhaps he will try somewhere else. Maybe someone else has even pushed him into it.

Some people are so convinced that God has called them that they see anybody who denies it, or even dares to challenge it, as a threat. They have made up their mind to become a priest; this is what God wants them to be, end of discussion! It is nobody else's business, they have no right to interfere. At the other extreme, there are men – admittedly very few – who leave the decision up to you. They will agree with whatever you say, provided they can do something in the Church. Finally, there are impulsive applications, along the lines of 'last week I suddenly knew I should be a priest'. Very seldom (fortunately) even the mother will call to apply on behalf of her son!

The vast majority of people who knock at our door have already travelled a long way and thought hard. Men of a certain age look before they leap. They may have walked around with the idea for years, but to their own irritation they have avoided coming to a decision. They may have been held back by something: an acquired position, a social status he is not ready to give up. He may have personal doubts: can I do it, am I really worthy to take on the responsibilities of ordained ministry?

The prospect of taking a new direction, going through a formation process, being under the direction of someone else, is not attractive. There is fear of the unknown. You have friends and you value their respect. What will they say? Just to say you are thinking of becoming a priest links you to an institution that, to put it mildly, is not exactly fashionable.

After a few years in the world of work, a man has acquired a degree of autonomy and is used to making his own decisions. Deep down some men know what they should do, and they know that one day they will just do it. But moving on can mean moving out of an established comfort zone; and that can be distinctly uncomfortable.[35] Some men talk about their sense of vocation all the time; others never mentioned it to anyone and the initial interview may well be the first time they have even attempted to articulate the possibility.

The most mature candidate is someone who, in faith and inner freedom, is prepared into enter a process of reflection on vocation and accepts the advice of an experienced mentor or Spiritual Director. Ideally this attitude of open enquiry will continue throughout the period from initial interview to the time the Church official recognises and endorses his call to ordained ministry.

A former student, now a highly respected priest, used to say at the end of each academic year: 'I am surprised every time that I am still here at the end of the year. You know, I don't have to be a priest; I am quite happy living my faith the way I do! I am heavily involved in different lay roles in my parish, I have a nice house, a good job; I've made it! But when I see parishes without a priest, and think about the urgent need for more clergy; and when I think I can do it, and you think I can, than I have to give it a go'. This is an ideal case. A student like this grows naturally towards ordination, and the faithful community grows equally naturally towards accepting him.

People like this are obviously suitable. Their life has been a positive process and development. They have demonstrated their vocation in their faith community through their active

---

[35] Compare, for example, the story of the rich young man in Mt. 19, 16-22

participation, their pastoral interest, and their personal attitude. Other people in the parish and pastors have often already wondered why they have not committed themselves to ordination earlier. These are the ones we can truly call *viri probati*, men who have proved themselves. Oddly enough, they are usually the candidates who do not consider themselves *worthy* and have not come forward earlier for that very reason. The ideal candidate is someone of whom it could be said: 'given his faith and personal attitude he could be ordained tomorrow; he just needs to acquire some pastoral skills'.

Even so, those responsible for formation must always keep their eyes open even with candidates who appear to be entirely suitable. It is not unknown for even the most obvious candidates to run into problems. This may be because the candidate has been loaded with unrealistic expectations from his parish where he may have been encouraged and admired. He may never have had the experience of failing, and therefore may not discover his real limitations until they become evident in formation. He may come to recognise aspects of himself he never knew before. Even so, in my experience, the problems that surface in such circumstances tend to be spiritual rather than psychological and therefore not too complex.

It takes time to arrive at the right decision. The candidate himself must feel the fruits of the Spirit are taking root in every aspect of his life, whereas those responsible for training must feel that the good tree can be recognised by its fruits.[36] The crucial issue is that the candidate and those responsible for his formation come to share a common understanding of what constitutes a genuine Christian calling. This search for common meaning leads back inevitably, I believe, to the vocation narratives in Sacred Scripture and their application in the tradition of the Church.

What follows in the next section applies not only to a vocation to ordained ministry but to other vocations and callings in life as well. It also applies to men and women of all ages.

---

[36] 'But the fruit of the Spirit is love, joy, peace, patience, kindness, goodness, faithfulness, gentleness, self-control.' (Gal 5,22). 'As for what was sown on good soil, this is he who hears the word and understands it; he indeed bears fruit'(Mt 13,19-23).

Talking about vocation

There are two ways of talking about vocation, two ways by which we can come to understand what it is. You can start with your own life, look at it with the eyes of faith, and tell it in the language of faith. Alternatively, you can start with a vocation narrative in Sacred Scripture, analyze it and describe it. Scripture does not use abstract language, it tells a story. On a pastoral level it is best to answer the question 'What is a vocation?' with a story, a narrative, either one's own or a biblical one. Abstract answers and general concepts generally help no one, least of all the candidate, who may not yet be able to articulate his inner experience, especially in an initial interview.

Even so, a candidate will often appear to have no difficulty in talking about his call to priesthood. He will speak of a desire to 'serve' and 'to be there for people', vague words that point to inner feelings and aspirations. Some candidates will refer to a particular event, a time or place where 'it happened'. It can be painful to focus on this event - the experience might have been too intense to yield to easy description. Applicants can feel annoyed if the interviewer persistently returns to probe the experience, as if to imply the candidate lacks an adequate understanding. This requires patience on the part of the formation director because it is of utmost importance that candidates reach a point where they can speak maturely about such experiences, even if it takes years to get there.

There is more to Christian vocation than a call to priesthood, or the diaconate, or the religious life, even though this is the focus of this particular book. Vocation needs to be seen in the broadest possible sense: 'everyone is called!'[37] We think of the vocation to life, to live as a human being, as a believer in the wider community. This demands respect for the many different ways in which people shape their lives in terms of human dignity, human rights, respect for the individual and for the community.

We are born into a community and we become part of that community. A distinctively Christian community is built around

---

[37] See the Final document of the European Congress on Vocations, *New Vocations for a New Europe.*, Kerkelijke Documentatie 121, Issue 27 No. 1, February, 1999. See also M. Ham, Presenting the Document *NVNE*, on 23 October 1998 in Hoeven (revised in 2003), http://www.pdob.nl/algemeen/pubenlezingen.htm

relationships rooted in the Trinitarian love of the Father, the Son and the Holy Spirit. This kind of community requires a de-centering of self, the kind of gradual detachment which enables the individual to rise and place themselves within a new context. The call to be one People lies close to the heart of the Old Testament but reaches a climax in the New Testament where the community of God's people becomes the *ecclesia*.

Scripture uses many terms and images to describe the vocation of God's People: living stones, holy nation, holy community, heritage, and the chosen nation. Each of us is called to be a living stone within and for this edifice. 'One becomes a member of God's people through faith and baptism, and to this community all men and women are called so that they may be one household, one People.'[38] The people of God are made up of the men and women who are called to be part of the *ecclesia*. But next to the communal vocation of Christians is the calling of each individual person. This is what we will now consider.

Introduction to the biblical spirituality of the individual Christian Vocation

The individual call

Each human life has meaning and needs meaning. It is a fundamental scriptural assumption that everyone needs to discover the meaning of his or her life. True meaning in life is something we discover, not something we create. For this reason it is better to speak of discovery of meaning than giving a meaning. It means discovering our very own personal calling. Life becomes meaningful when we discover our personal calling and strive to respond. The life and the future of God's people is to a large extent determined by the way individual men and women fulfil their personal calling.

Biblical call narratives mostly concern people who are already adults and usually convey a sense of glory, heroism, and solemnity. The intention is to make an impression on those who first heard these stories and invite their imitation. It seems clear to me that the reality may have been somewhat less spectacular than the story might suggest.

---

[38] Catechism of the Catholic Church, 804.

These call narratives were often written many years after the event, frequently at times when God's people were going through times of crisis. The author wanted to highlight important characters in the past, to show how they saved their people. The intention was that those who heard these stories might find the faith to interpret their own experience with courage and hope, as they looked to the past to hear the prophets and others with a special vocation speak the Word of God.

Prophets do not usually try to please their audience. Sometimes, they appear even abrasive as they challenge the people of God. Yet at the same time they can feel deeply unworthy of their calling. The more they are aware of the high responsibility of speaking the Word of God, the more humbly they will seek to avoid claiming their own benefit or glory.

Common elements in Bible narratives

Biblical call narratives tend to share common elements. The Old Testament speaks, for example, of the call of Abraham, Joseph, Moses, Joshua, Gideon, Samson, Samuel, Saul, David, Elijah, Isaiah, Jeremiah, Ezekiel, Hosea, Amos, and Jonah. The New Testament mentions the call of John the Baptist, Jesus, Mary, Mary Magdalene, the 12 disciples, the 72, Matthias, the seven deacons, Barnabas and Paul, and Timothy. The process in the contemporary Church remains much the same: we could even add our own names to the list of those who are called!

All of these stories are different. Yet the biblical narratives invite us to consider if there are any common elements: what kind of people or communities were called? What kind of events led to the call? What were the tasks given? And so on.

In fact, nearly all of these narratives share certain themes:

- God's word is addressed to a particular person,
- There is a guarantee.
- There is a mission.
- There is an initial reaction of the person who is called.
- The vocation has a subject.
- There is an object.
- There are other persons or groups involved.
- There is the socio-economic, religious or political context.

- There is a question: why someone is called?
- There is another question: what is the purpose of the call?

These components come together to form a picture of each unique vocation, including our own. Although we cannot imitate the life of others, we can often see that our own stories reflect a similar pattern of being called and sent. We are able, therefore, to lay our own book of life next to the Book of Life.

Looking at vocation as a process

The subject and object of vocation

It is always God (the Lord, YHWH, or an Angel sent by God) who calls. It is always a human being who is called. We should not say therefore that somebody *has* a vocation, but that someone is *given,* or even, '*suffer*' a vocation. In other words, it is something that happens to them. True vocation is never ours; it is given by God and can therefore be taken away again. Unlike ordination (or being a parent) which cannot be undone, mission or jurisdiction can be withdrawn. In the same way, skills or qualities acquired in a previous way of life may not necessarily be taken into the priesthood.

Many priests, deacons or religious never use again the professional skills acquired in the course of their former employment. A cook will not necessarily continue as cook in a religious community and an organist who has become a priest will not play the organ during Mass. In fact those skills are to be left behind. A new life and occupation is opening out, with a different goal, new concerns and a different purpose. Belonging to the Lord can mean, and often will mean, walking down unexpected and unfamiliar paths, not pursuing your own goals but following Christ in obedience, poverty and with a selfless, pure heart. What is needed is a readiness to adapt: for example, a teacher who becomes a priest will certainly make use of his pedagogical skills when teaching the catechism. But if preaching turns into a lecture, his teaching skills have become an obstacle to ministry and something he must learn to use overcome.[39]

---

[39] This is an issue which obviously invites significant further discussion. The basic idea that originally lay behind the Bovendonk project was the notion that men could become priests, (or, later, deacons) 'from their profession'. But what does this actually mean, both in theory and in practice? There are many

Man receives the call. It does not belong to him as of right, it is given to him for the benefit of others. It is God who calls, the Lord, JHWH, an Angel of the Lord. In the New Testament it is Jesus or the Holy Spirit. Vocation always has a Trinitarian dimension, and it is always directed towards a community. The dynamics of vocation involve not a dialogue but a 'trialogue': God-person-people. Without people (Church) there can be no vocation. To say that one wants to serve other people but not the Church does not make any sense. It is a *contradictio in terminis*. People who say this, confuse 'Church' and 'hierarchy'. They forget that Church is simply shorthand for 'God's people, of whom I am a member'. Nor must we forget that vocation is always rooted in a concrete historical situation, a specific time and a specific place. It is always related to specific needs. Usually God will call somebody who lives precisely in that context, rarely somebody from outside. It can happen, but only because somebody is needed from outside that particular community to point them beyond themselves.

---

examples in scripture of people in a job or profession (shepherd, fisherman, tax collector) who are called from that position to take on a new vocation, and often they are required to leave everything behind, including their established skills, in order to follow the Lord. Sometimes they go back to their former occupations after finishing their particular mission. Paul made tents so that he would not be a burden on the Christian communities. In the present situation the Church expects priests to devote their entire life to what Msgr. Ernst calls, the work of the Faith. Some dioceses want their deacons to be full-time employed in the Church, others expect deacons to earn a living and serve as deacons in their spare time. If the expression 'from one's profession' means using existing professional skills and qualifications in ministry, then this could cause serious misunderstanding. Rather, at Bovendonk the expression was taken to mean that during the first four years of training, the candidate moves between the two worlds of work and formation, gradually appropriating the new way of life of a priest or a deacon. The idea is that the future minister should be able to function in a new role without being estranged from the ordinary secular world around him. These first four years also allow the student to test his vocation without burning his bridges. Four years should be enough for the student and for those responsible for his formation to determine the right way forward. Only when such an assessment has been made should the student be asked to give up his professional employment and enter into a full-time pastoral placement. There is a real danger in trying too hard to 'use' the skills of the former profession. In fact, nobody quite knows how to do that anyway. But having said that, perhaps we instinctively focus too much on how we want the future ordained minister to perform and on the spirituality of the priest or deacon as we perceive it. Perhaps we have not looked quite hard enough at the experiences and resources our candidates bring with them, as Worthen and Snijders suggest in their contributions elsewhere in this volume.

God's people, the *ecclesia*, is therefore a key stakeholder in every vocation narrative. This gives the Church has a major voice in the discernment process, preventing the sense of vocation from drifting away into a subjective, romantic and private spirituality, something between God and the individual with no space for anyone else. In the final analysis, the person is called to mediate the grace of God for the benefit of others. This is made very clear in Jeremiah 1, 7: 'To all to whom I send you, you shall go and whatever I command you, you shall speak'.

The *object* of God's call is also specifically summonsed by name (Moses, Saul... you). A personal relation is thus established that touches the very core of that person's humanity, frequently shown in quite physical terms. So the experience of God can be accompanied by trembling, fainting, crying, not being able to eat or drink, temporary paralysis, blindness or deafness.[40] This change in a person can be so profound that it actually leads in Scripture to a name change (Abraham, Sarah, Peter).

This was, and sometimes still is, the reason why a different name is taken by those joining a monastic order or the novitiate of a religious congregation. Assuming a different name signifies that the person in question is committed to a different way of living, that he or she is changing his or her way of life, a change that will affect the very core of their being. It means giving up who and what one has been, a commitment that leaves no room for turning back. St. Paul puts it this way: 'if I preach the Gospel, that gives me no ground for boasting, for necessity is laid upon me. Woe to me if I do not preach the Gospel. For if I do this of my own will, I have a reward; but if not of my own will, I am entrusted with a stewardship (1Cor. 9: 16-17).'

This seems to contradict what was said above about the *trialogue* and the importance of an authorative role for others in the vocation narrative. Paul was profoundly convinced of his personal call from the Lord, to go to the non-Jews. Still he first put it to Peter, the *primus inter pares*, who, in the first instance, did not approve at all. Paul recognized Peter's authority by asking for his agreement; Peter eventually recognized the authenticity of Paul's vocation, gave him his blessing and sent him on his mission.

---

[40] See, for example, Dan. 10; Is. 21; Ezek. 8,3; Acts 9

Go, I send you and I will vouch for you

The idea of a journey is a recurring feature in all vocation narratives. 'Go, I send you, I shall be with you, I will bless you, 'I am with you to deliver you' (Jer. 1, 8). The person who is called leaves with the warrant: God-with-us. He has to do something specific, he has to get moving. It follows that *vocation* is a synonym for *mission*. One is given a task and what matters is not what the person called feels about the assignment, but whether the job is done.

In many biblical narratives, the first reaction is often one of resistance or complaint, an attempt to present excuses in order to avoid the task in hand: I cannot speak because I stammer, I am too young, and so forth. The person who is called tries to find a way to get out of the demanding work ahead. In spite of these protestations, however, most set out in the end to fulfil the mission entrusted to them. The Gospel does not depend on the individual in any case, but on the grace of God who takes all kinds of people in all sorts of situations, and uses them to fulfil His plan. In other words, by assuming our role in God's purpose we participate in building up the Body of Christ (I Cor. 12).

It should be self-evident that a faithful person will participate in the Christian community and actively contribute to the well-being of the Church. We speak of 'volunteers', but strictly speaking committed and active members are not 'volunteers'. The sharing of personal gifts, charisms and talents on behalf of the Body of Christ is not a voluntary activity but a basic ministry which follows from baptism, assumed and developed after confirmation and admission to the Blessed Sacrament. There are no volunteers in the Church, only those who have been called by God and given a job.

Why me?

The reason a particular individual is called, and the purpose of that call, is always intrinsically linked to a specific historical context. Nobody is called for his or her own sake. The call is always for the benefit of God's people in a particular situation. People pray for delivery, they complain of their misery, they cry out to heaven. They feel trapped in a situation, and God does not want it to continue. A merciful God hears the cry of his people and sends somebody to deliver them. Why this person and not another is a question usually left unanswered in the scriptural narratives.

A person is not called because of intelligence, beauty, strength, shrewdness or whatever. The reasons for each calling belong to God alone and God keeps that to himself: 'O Lord, thou hast searched me and known me! Thou knowest when I sit down and when I rise up; thou discernest my thoughts from afar' (Psalm 139, 1). The personal qualities of the one who is called are of minor importance. We can only guess at the "why?" of the call because this is hidden in God's love. Some are relieved when they finally realise this truth: the question is no longer important. But the biblical narratives suggest that others are not happy to live with the unknowing and keep searching for an answer..

These tend to be men with a problem-solving approach to life who in pastoral situations will not be afraid to give answers, even when people ask profoundly difficult questions such as: why this illness, why this suffering, why death? Being able to answer such questions gives them a feeling of assurance, of being in control. Not having an answer, not knowing, makes them feel powerless and insecure, perhaps even a failure. Sometimes such people need to learn that being able to accept the mysteries of God enhances our trust in Him. It means giving yourself away. It creates inner freedom.

The 'finality' of a vocation lies in the concrete situation

But if the question 'why me' remains largely unanswered, the purpose of a call is usually pretty clear in the biblical narratives. In Scripture, the reasons given may be that God's people are oppressed, that they have become unfaithful to JHWH, that the land is suffering from socio-economic abuse, that faith is disappearing, that people are beset by illness or natural disasters, peoples or countries live in ways that are not in accordance with the reign of God, and so on.[41] These are always concrete situations facing real people. God names the circumstances that are not acceptable to Him and calls someone to rescue the people from oppression. We could say therefore

---

[41] The kingdom of God does not mean food and drink, but righteousness and peace and joy in the Holy Spirit (Rom 14.17)

that a calling from God is always rooted in a response to a particular situation.

These situations do not have to be grand or dramatic; the face of Christ can be defiled by little things as well. But because a vocation is neither self-generated nor given for its own sake, we must be cautious in adopting subjective criteria to test its authenticity. The initiative lies with God. The vocation uses the person who is called but is aimed at others. No one is given a beautiful voice just to sing in the bathroom. The voice is given to praise the Lord and to carry other people along.

To be complete, a vocation to work in a particular situation must be recognised and accepted by the person called. He must enter the arena, stand in its midst, and on behalf of the Lord commit himself to address the situation: convert the people, relieve their suffering or whatever he is called to do. It is precisely *this* situation which cries for a remedy - more justice, freedom, God - even if nobody is able to put this neatly into words. In the cry itself, or in the anguish that lies behind it, we see the defiled face of the Christ who invites us to respond:

Lord, when did we see thee hungry and feed thee, or thirsty and give thee drink? And when did we see thee a stranger and welcome thee, or naked and clothe thee? And when did we see thee sick or in prison and visit thee? (...) Truly I say to you, as you did it to one of the least, of these my brethren, you did it to me. (Mt. 25, 37b-40).

The concrete situation to which each person is called will sooner or later become clear through the discernment process. The individual will become more aware of an ability to do something about this or that and this will help him to become more objective and articulate about his vocation. One man may lie awake because of a crisis of faith among his people, another may feel a pull to deal with a socio-economic situation, whilst another may feel called to alleviate the physical or psychological sufferings of his fellow men. One man may lose worry about the lack of priests, another about the suffering in third world countries, and yet another may feel deeply concerned about the plight of immigrants. A man's vocation can most likely be discovered where he feels most involved. That he is touched by this or that situation is a good indication of what he is called to. Others may be aware of the problem but not feel personally addressed by it in anything like the same degree.

It is possible therefore that a man's vocation in life may overlap with his profession. That is especially likely if the *cry* of the other person means more to me than my own well-being. Self-fulfilment may be important but it is rarely enough to induce a person with a vocation to commit himself. True happiness and personal achievement are, in my opinion, side-effects of working for a cause. Self-fulfilment is never the primary purpose in a truly vocational sense. This is a challenge for the counsellor.

It is possible to experience a sense of inner call, but this experience can in fact disguise a deeper subconscious drive to satisfy an unfulfilled need. Many people need to be *needed.* They generally have low self-esteem but feel a sense of affirmation when others ask them for help. They are often unknowingly dependent on the dependency of others. To desire to be a support for others may be a good public reason for seeking to be ordained, but it can be misleading. The real motive may not be as unselfish as it appears. If such men are not regularly affirmed in ministry they easily become frustrated, and this invariably has a negative impact on their pastoral work.

There may be many examples of subconscious drivers that need bringing to the surface during the discernment process. I do not mean that only people with the purest of intentions can become priests: who can genuinely say that he really has no secondary purpose wrapped up with the best of his intentions? But when somebody says he wants to serve others, it is important to be aware of these deeper possible motives so that the person concerned can learn to manage them. To use the words of St. John the Baptist: 'He must increase, but I must decrease' (John 3,30). In other words, the objective, evangelical motives in us must grow stronger, and the subjective, often self-directed motives must not be allowed to dominate.

Seen in this way, vocation is not a vague concept; it has hands and feet. It is a concrete event, a dynamic movement freeing oneself from what is less than satisfactory and allowing something better to emerge. It means moving one, leaving Egypt and setting out for the Promised Land - stepping out of a sinful situation, on the way to holiness or wholeness in God. The true prophet not only denounces but also points towards another future, one which is in accordance with God's plan of salvation.

Other aspects

This essay does not attempt to touch on many other aspects of religious vocation. What about the contemplative vocation, for instance, which on the surface has little to offer active pastoral engagement or social action? Yet it is precisely these contemplative orders which are most profoundly connected with the world through prayer. Vocation is always more than activity of any kind: it involves many other things. To name but one other possible source of tension, vocation involves a call to obedience within the Church which can cause real problems when leaders and those who owe them obedience differ fundamentally in their understanding of what needs to be done.

Then there are questions of priority: which comes first – the call to service or the call to celibacy? How does priestly vocation relate to religious vocation? What has priority for the married deacon, his family or his ministry? Why is the Holy Sacrament so important? Does the Lord's call *'Come and follow me'* mean that we should begin a journey without knowing where it will lead? What should I do (vocational choice) when I feel attracted to very different situations?

All these questions and many more require a separate volume. The focus at the moment is on the prior question of psychological motivation. The Church needs to be as objective as possible when engaged in the process of discernment and avoid being pulled into conversations which operate only at the surface with the subjective rationale for vocation presented by the candidate. No serious discernment process can be satisfied with a well-intentioned 'I feel I have to do this'. True vocation requires a high degree of honesty to probe one's motives more objectively.

The role of prayer in the vocation narratives

Vocation is about a specific charge that is given to each of us in life. The issue is simply 'what does the Lord require of me?' This question can only be answered when there is a personal relationship with God rooted in prayer and grace - the initiative always remains with God. God's Word can best be heard in the silence of meditative and contemplative prayer. It is in prayer that we learn to listen to and converse with God and to guide our feet into the way of the Lord.[42]

In prayer we take all our thoughts, reflections and knowledge with us, including comments and advice others have offered in response to our own personal discernment. Often, and especially in the early stages of discernment, the question 'Lord what do You want me to do?' should be considered carefully with the support of an experienced Spiritual Director. There wisdom and experience can help to fine-tune our openness to the voice of the Lord. It will strengthen our inner disposition to listen as we grow in our capacity to respond 'speak, Lord, for your servant listens'.

This prayerful process may take years[43] though it is possible that some spiritual experiences can be so overwhelming that the response is almost immediate. As the call becomes clearer much then depends on the hearer. How does he respond? The process of hearing and responding has been well described by the Carmelite Wilfried Stinissen, in his little book *Mary in Scripture and in our Life*. He writes:

> 'When praying the *Angelus,* the message of the Angel with its threefold structure of our human relationship with God: God's invitation, the answer that the human being gives, and the fruit, which is the living tangible presence of God, is manifested in us.'[44]

Mary's *Fiat* resulted directly in the Incarnation of the Word, in the Word becoming flesh. In a similar way something can only happen in a situation where we become aware of the absence of God or where we see the suffering Christ and are able freely to say 'yes' to God's summons. The Word will only become flesh again if those who are called accept God's gracious invitation. The face of the suffering Christ will only be healed to the extent that the person called commits himself and follows through on that commitment. In all freedom we must say 'yes'. If we say 'No' nothing can or will happen.

---

[42] Cf. I Kings 19

[43] Cf. Afonso, H., S.J., *The Personal Vocation*, Ed. Pontificia Università Gregoriana, Rome 1989.

[44] Stinissen, W., O. Carm, *Maria in de Bijbel en in ons Leven,* Carmelitana, Gent, 1983, p. 7

Much of this will become clearer as the candidate matures in terms of spirituality and learns to discern the spirits. Without prayer, it is impossible to know what the Lord is asking. This prayer will not be that of the praying person alone, since it is the Spirit who prays in us. It is therefore also the duty of those who accompany candidates and are responsible for their formation to pray with them. How else can they assess the authenticity of the candidate's vocation and give a credible advice about their suitability for ordination?

Man is called in freedom, for freedom

The biblical vocation narratives make clear that the Lord does not look for slavish subservience but for free human beings. No one is forced to follow Him. Christ invites: 'come and see'. The decision to follow Christ is not forced and the person always remains free to reconsider. The extent to which people are genuinely free to make decisions and implement them varies from one person or situation to another. For example, a person full of inner conflict is not as free as someone who is more settled. Freedom in the Christian sense of the word means one is able to stand before God as a partner in the new covenant.[45]

With the help of grace, humanity is free to engage in a responsible way, and within limits, in a vocational dialogue with God. But we can never be completely sure how free each decision really is. As Rulla puts it, 'the question therefore is not whether a human being is free but rather whether or not and to what degree and in which way he can exercise his freedom.'[46]

Everyone is called within the limits of the internal freedom he possesses at a particular time. It would seem that God always respects the psychological laws that govern human behaviour, rules he Himself has instituted. Therefore everyone, by his own effort, must find proper ways to enhance this inner freedom. The individual person is clearly master over aspects of the self, and for that part he is responsible. Further, those who would seek to guide others to freedom in Christ must themselves be growing in that freedom.

---

[45] Jer. 31,31; Ez. 36,26

[46] Rulla, L., S.J., *Anthropology of the Christian Vocation*, Vol. I, Gregorian University Press, Rome 1986, p. 23.

The universal 'royal priesthood' (1 Peter 2: 9) given in baptism enables, even requires us to:

- live as free human beings, free of external duress and especially free of internal forces that restrain us from living the Gospel values that we opt for. That is our primary mission, our first assignment in life.
- live in authentic community (*communio, koinonia*) with the universe, the world, the created order.
- be there for others - to help build the Kingdom of God so that God's plan of salvation becomes a reality through *diaconia* or service. This is the new life celebrated and shown through the *liturgy*.

In the next chapter we will consider the response to God's call, to God's invitation and commission. The purpose of this chapter is to consider other issues that may need to be addressed during the preliminary interview stage so that the candidate can live into his vocation more effectively in full awareness of the processes that play a part in his journey to ordination. Such obstacles and limitations that a candidate may experience need to be acknowledged and dealt with if they are not to hold him back.

7. RESPONDING WITH INCREASING INNER FREEDOM

By Matt Ham

> *...any institution which, in pursuing its own basic principles, does not seek to render explicit its own anthropological view, will inevitably end up by accepting the views of others, especially those which are more fashionable.*[47]

Introduction

The last chapter looked at the vocational process from the perspective of biblical spirituality. This exercise clarified that in the dialogue between God and humanity, it is always God who takes the initiative and it is up to the individual person to respond to God's invitation, to His call, and to accept the mission He assigns. God not only makes a covenant with His people, He invites every individual person to enter into a personal relationship with Him. In this chapter we will focus on the human being who responds, who accepts the invitation to form a personal relationship with God and who tries to give that relationship more depth.

A personal relationship with God is established through a commitment to follow Jesus Christ, who is 'the way, and the truth, and the life' (Jn. 14,6) with a pure, humble and obedient heart. In practice, this means becoming more Christlike in word and deed, in what we do and do not do. As we advance along this road, we inevitably bump up against our own limitations and the diverse particularities that are part of our human condition.

If we are serious about our desire to be more like Jesus Christ, we discover that we are often not free to do what we want. Some people feel these constraints more than others, but nobody is ever totally free in this life. Our relationship with God, in and through Jesus Christ, becomes deeper, richer in meaning and more loving as both partners in the relationship come to stand freely before one another. God, of course, is totally free. It is we

---

[47] Rulla, L.M., S.J. *Anthropology of the Christian Vocation: Vol I, Interdisciplinary Bases*, Gregorian University Press, Rome, 1986, p.18.

who, by the grace of God, are given the capacity to grow into this inner freedom.

This formation is always the work of a life-time. It does not stop until that time when we are wholly taken up into the freedom of God. The kind and quality of our human relationships are a reflection of our relationship with God, and *vice versa*. We learn more about ourselves from our interactions with other people. It is also with the help of others that we develop the relationship with Jesus Christ that brings us closer to God. Communities of faith made up of people committed to developing spiritually and growing in holiness will always build up a variety of gifts (cf. I Cor. 12).

The priesthood and the diaconate are two of these gifts. Priests and deacons are called to be both shepherds and members of the flock in order to be able to lead faith communities *and* individuals through their own process of sanctification. For that very reason, one of the primary responsibilities of clergy is to increase their understanding of the human condition and gain as much self-awareness as possible. As we set about doing this, it is important to remember that in the end it is God who has things in hand.

The themes discussed in this chapter apply specifically to candidates for the priesthood and the diaconate but are *mutatis mutandis* also applicable to other vocations. The substance of this chapter largely consists of the content of the second course I gave to first year students at Bovendonk. Keep in mind while reading this chapter that, when I speak of 'values', I refer to qualities that are directly or indirectly the result of our freely-made decision to follow Jesus Christ in all that we do, while at the same time being informed by the Christian tradition as taught by the *Magisterium* (teaching office) of the Church.

The limitations of the human condition are inherent

The path that leads individual candidates towards priestly or diaconal formation can follow different routes. Some arrive already deeply convinced that they have been called, while others are more hesitant and hope to test the authenticity of their vocation through the formation process itself. Conversations with candidates show that the sense of vocation is often based on an intuition, a 'kind of (confident) knowing', or a religious experience. Sometimes, the final push comes from people around them. Sometimes it comes in the form of an overwhelming experience which can last for a brief or long time. Some candidates become very emotional when talking about their choice to become priest or deacon while others remain cool and rational.

Some walk around for years with the thought of seeking Holy Orders in their head while others have only struggled with the question for a few weeks. Some return to experiences and aspirations from the time they were children or young adults and finally decide it is time to turn an old ideal into reality. And yet others, have set out on a different journey in search of a deeper meaning in life or a more profound spirituality, and in the process have discovered a call to Holy Orders.

Biblical narratives and church history both show that the people whom God calls never come from a stereotypical background with a predictable set of experiences. God calls whom He wills. For that reason every aspirant who feels called to Holy Orders must to be taken seriously. It is a daunting responsibility to enter into a conversation between God and the potential aspirant. No one should judge or dismiss this lightly.

At the same time we need to remember that biblical narratives as well as the tradition of the Church, never consider religious vocation to be a private affair. There is always a third party involved, even when God calls upon a 'stranger', an outsider, to give direction to His people. His call is always related to a specific community, place and time. So vocation involves other people – the whole people of God have a responsibility to promote ministerial vocation, with the bishop taking the final decision in the case of ordination.[48]

From the perspective of the Church this means that there must always be someone else involved in the discernment of vocation; someone who can stand back and form a more objective opinion. The role of the Church is not to question the idea that God might be calling that person, but rather to assess the suitability of a candidate for ordained ministry using the criteria laid down by the Church, as spelled out in the relevant official documents.[49]

---

[48] Ordination rite for Deacons, Priests and Bishops. If a married man is ordained to the diaconate his spouse has to give her official consent.

From the candidate's point of view, it is crucial that his vocation is recognized and affirmed by the Church. Even more fundamental than this 'external' affirmation, however, is his inner conviction about the genuineness of his calling. I mean by this that the candidate has been able through his prayer and spirituality to place himself willingly in a position of obedience to the will of God. This openness alone will enable him to surrender himself in a way that leads both to personal fulfilment and succeed in an effective mission. It is enough that the candidate should want this willing obedience; complete self-surrender, after all, is the work of a lifetime.

When this openness is given a solid foundation has been laid. The determination to strive for holiness and the intention to cooperate with God's grace are transformed into action step-by-step, despite the inevitable setbacks that come along. In the ordination liturgy for the priesthood, the bishop asks the ordinand 'Are you prepared to assist the bishops, to preside over the community, to preach the Word of God with dedication, and to commit yourself ever more to Christ?' The candidate answers every question with, 'Yes, I will', not 'Yes, I guarantee it'. There are no guarantees, and both the bishop and the person being ordained have to make do with a simple 'Yes, I will'. If the one being ordained is prepared to continue to grow, God can more easily fulfil His work in that person.

But on the other hand, we also know from experience that good intentions are rarely enough to promote freedom and commitment in vocation. It is part of the human condition to be hemmed in by forces we can never completely control. Paul recognizes this struggle in himself, when he writes 'I do not understand my own actions; for I do not do what I want, but I do the very thing I hate and I delight in the law of God, in my inmost self, but I see in my members another law at war with the law of

---

[49] See, for example: the conciliar decree *Presbyterorum Ordinis* (1965); the decree *Optatum Totius* (1965). The Code of Canon Law (1983) and Pope John Paul II: *Pastores DaboVobis* (1992). From the Congregation for Catholic Education we have the *Ratio Fundamentalis Institutionis Sacerdotalis* (1970, revised in 1985) and many other documents. From the Congregation for the Clergy there is: *The Priest, Pastor and Leader of the parochial community* (2002). From the Congregation for Divine Worship and Sacraments: *Investigating the suitability of candidates for ordination (1997)*.

my mind and making me captive to the law of sin which dwells in my members' (Rom. 7,15; 22-23).

Gaudium et Spes (10) picks up on this: "The truth is that the imbalances under which the modern world labors are linked with that more basic imbalance which is rooted in the heart of man. For in man himself many elements wrestle with one another... Hence he suffers from internal divisions, and from these flow so many and such great discords in society."

This Pastoral Constitution suggests that it is not society that creates the inner conflicts, but on the contrary, it is the inner conflict in each human being that creates social division. It is therefore of the greatest importance to learn to deal with these inner conflicts. This is not only necessary for our own well-being but also to avoid the danger of those inner conflicts spilling over to cause discord and division around us.

The early Christian tradition provided us with the spiritual resources needed to help us master these inner conflicts. These are *lectio divina*, spiritual direction, prayer, active participation in a community of faith, and receiving the sacraments of the Church. Devotion to Mary, reading the lives of the saints, the practice of Christian virtues, penance and fasting, and other forms of spiritual discipline, could be added to that list.

For many people these spiritual aids are all that is needed. They have been sufficient e not only for well-known or declared saints, but also for countless unknown Christians, men and women, young and old, married and single, religious and priests. As they seek to imitate Christ in their lives, people such as these bear rich fruit in terms of pastoral care and effective witness. This in turn, by the grace of God, enables many others to come to Christ.

It appears however that quite a few of other people, without wanting to play down the spiritual fruitfulness of their lives, hardly make any real progress. Over and over again, they confess the same sins and constantly miss the target with regard to their relationship with God and neighbour, and are consequently tempted to lose hope. They lack direction in their spiritual lives. We all know of people who sincerely want to follow Christ and try their very best but run into powerful inner forces that override their conscious efforts. As a result, they behave in a way that is in direct contradiction to the very values they hold most central in the Christian life. This makes it all the more important that the focus should be on understanding the inner processes that motivate, influence or even direct such behaviour, instead of simply criticising their negative behaviour.

Conversion and vocation

Every vocational narrative includes moments when the person in question arrives at an insight that makes change possible. He wants to live differently, follow Christ more nearly, and give himself more fully on behalf of his neighbour. Values which he did not appreciate in the past now are considered important. God's grace, freely given, transforms his heart in such a way that it makes possible deepening understanding with regard to faith, contrition, prayer, lifestyle, priesthood or another vocation.

When these new values are internalized, a fresh challenge is presented, namely the integration of these values into one's entire life. But if that is to happen, there must first be a willingness to accept this change of direction and allow it to have a real impact on our lives. Only then can the process of *internalization* really begin.

Rulla briefly defined *internalization* as follows: 'I internalize a value revealed or lived by Christ insofar as I am ready and *free* to accept this value as leading me to a theocentric self-transcendence (rather than to an ego-centric or social-philanthropic self-transcendence), to be transformed by this value, and to do all this out of love for the intrinsic importance of this value, rather than for the subjective importance that this value may have for me (cf. Gal 2.20, with Rom 14, 7 – 8 and 2 Cor 5, 14 – 15).' (Rulla pp.433f)

From the perspective of priestly and diaconal formation, *internalization* thus requires:

- a degree of openness and internal freedom on the part of the person concerned which in turn is closely related to issues of maturity (the 'how')
- an understanding of the values revealed and lived by Christ (the 'what')
- a desire to love for nothing more than love's own intrinsic value (the 'why')

Rulla calls this process a 're-shaping in Christ' in three phases or three levels of spiritual practice. The first stage is the dialectical process described in the guidelines for discernment which are suggested for Week One of Ignatius' *Exercises* (313-327)[50]. A successful result would usually lead the person to choose virtue over sin.

According to the guidelines for Week Two (328-336) of the *Exercises* the second stage, is designed to encourage the person to choose that which is truly good rather than that which is only superficially attractive. Finally (Week Four), the person comes to a point of total surrender based on the love for God for God's own sake.

Being re-shaped means "being transformed by God through His Spirit in the altruistic love of Christ (Rulla, 270). This transformation consists of achieving a measure of collaboration with God and neighbour, letting go of self, and acquiring the ability to use oneself on behalf of others as well as the Other.

Healy points out that this description of the process of being called may seem like a linear one-way path that leads directly to union with God. In fact, from the perspective of the *Exercises*, this path is more like a spiral, a backwards and forwards movement between inner reflection and active engagement. The person on retreat is asked to consider how God is 'hard at work in all created things on this earth' and thus reflect on the basis of divine love (*Exercises*, 230 – 237), to. Ignatius thus implies that a new way of being joyfully engaged in the world is and must be possible.[51]

Moving beyond the Self: Self-transcendence

There are two ways in which we experience God's invitation or calling. The first one is that part of the human being which has the capacity and desire to grow beyond the self and turn to God by embodying Christian values and so cooperate with God's grace. The other concerns inherent human limitations that *can* obstruct grace. We always live with this tension.

---

[50] Ignatius van Loyola, *Spiritual Exercises,* Paulist Press, 1991.

[51] Healy, T., S.J., *The challenge of Self-transcendence: Anthropology of the Christian Vocation and Bernard Lonergan*, in: Imoda, F., S.J.,(ed.) *A Journey to Freedom,* Peeters, Leuven, 2000, 71-115.

Rulla's fundamental assumption is that, in spite of this inner tension, the person called is still capable of rising above the self in order to deepen his relationship with God and move towards Him. He (Rulla) calls this 'theocentric self-transcendence' or 'growing above oneself towards God'. In his *Method*[52] Lonergan depicts a similar four stage process which he describes as experiencing, understanding, judging and deciding. The first three steps towards this goal comprise acquisition of knowledge and the fourth one leads to decision and action.

The first step, *experiencing*, includes sensory perceptions and the powerful role that feelings, imagination, fantasy, emotional reactions or tendencies of attraction and repulsion play in what is perceived. Such experiences can arise both internally and externally. The second step on the way to making a decision involves coming to an *understanding* which leads to practical insight. This is not yet a full understanding of all that is going on but rather a sense of what *might* be done.

The third step, *judging*, consists of a critical evaluation of what is going on. The practical insight yielded by the second step leads to one or more possible options. This third step combines these practical and critical insights and so extends the sense of what is possible as well as increasing awareness of the basic motivations at work.

At this point we are able to explore not only the consequences of each option but also the drivers, that is to say the reasons we might be tempted to choose one way rather than another. Careful examination of these options leads us to another decision in terms of the action that needs to be taken to uphold the key values we cherish. This involves nothing more complicated than a simple listing of alternatives in terms of what is now perceived to be good and better, bad or worse.

The fourth and final step is the one of *responsibility and decision*. This has to do with coming to trust our judgement and so accept responsibility for our decisions. In this way, we move from evaluation to action. Decision-making is always based on value judgements which in turn prompt action. Sometimes conflict is generated as the individual struggles between 'ought' and 'is',

---

[52] Lonergan, B.J.F., *Method in Theology*, University of Toronto Press, 1990, Toronto, reprinted 1996, p. 238.

what they know they *ought* to do, and the contradiction of ingrained habit. Or sometimes, the enormity of the decision may seem so overwhelming that the individual will simply adopt an avoidance strategy and keep putting it off.

In his *Method* (p. 19) Lonergan underlines the importance of this functional analysis of understanding and decision-making. Each step in the process builds on and completes the previous one. But each step can also carry with it the mistakes and imperfections already present in previous step. This is particularly true with the mistakes and imperfections that were unacknowledged because they were beyond the range of our conscious awareness and which therefore remain active for that very reason.

No serious progress is possible until each step has been properly negotiated; those who try to short-circuit the process will quickly find that they are simply brought back to square one. This happens time and time again, particularly if weaknesses remain unacknowledged or unnoticed. Unconscious needs or suppressed and painful psychological drivers are frequently the most difficult issues to discern.

In the right circumstances an adult may make a conscious decision to deal with uncomfortable psychological realities. The decision to attend to them, however, is almost certainly also driven by the unconscious, a key part of the human psyche which needs to be clearly acknowledged and accepted.

It cannot be emphasized enough that emotions, and certainly unconscious emotions, influence and shape in different ways the processes that lead to making judgments and decisions[53] (Rulla, pp. 142-143). A simple example would be the way small children learn to react to being thirsty. The child senses a lack of bodily fluid, which he or she learns to call *thirst*. The child then sees a bottle of fluid in the kitchen is drawn towards it and drinks the content.

The child jumps from need to action and skips the crucial stage of questioning what might be inside the bottle. It could be bleach or a dishwashing liquid, but the small child does not know

---

[53] For a more complete treatment of this question in relation to ethics see Kiely, B.M, S.J., *Psychology and Moral Theology*, Gregorian University Press, Rome, 1980, pp. 136-170.

enough to ask whether this particular fluid is dangerous. An adult, on the other hand, has (probably!) learned to insert one other step into the process. The adult also feels the need for a drink, is equally drawn to the bottle, but then stops to investigate before taking a drink. Otherwise, disaster could easily follow as careless adults quickly discover.

Lonergan understands this process of four steps to be a natural consequence of human curiosity and the drive to discover the surrounding world. We ask questions, we try to understand, we ask ourselves what to do and how we can act responsibly. This tendency belongs to what may be called the innate drive to rise above the self, that is to say the need to keep on going. This is one of the positive aspects of human spontaneity.

The positive trait of conscious and intentional self-transcendence in turn is manifested in three separate phases: knowledge, morality and love. The four steps of experiencing, understanding, judging and believing make it possible to make an assessment of reality and transcend the conditioned naiveté of 'I recognize it, I have experienced it, and therefore it is true' without being swayed by personal preference. Openness to the truth invites movement beyond the self and leads to what might be called cognitive self-transcendence.

Another way to determine what might be the truth in any given situation is to ask 'and what should I do now?' This question opens out the next phase of cognitive *moral* self-transcendence. The way is thus prepared for the third phase of love, when 'the isolation of the individual is broken, and he functions not only for himself but also for the good of others'. (Rulla p. 144)

What is the purpose of self-transcendence?

Self-transcendence is never an end in itself. It is always related to the greater purpose or designated goal perceived to have value in itself. In other words, we seek to rise above ourselves for the sake of a quality such as truth, or the virtue of self-transcendence, or the affirmation of the Other or others out of love. There always has to be another point of reference beyond ourselves that has value in itself. This could be a worthwhile project, a cause worth defending or the encouragement of someone we love. When choosing to act in such a manner, we are making a decision. Such a decision has the effect of transcending as well as denying ourselves.

It is natural to ask: What is really the point of denying the self? This is a normal, healthy question (Healy, p. 82). What is achieved by self-transcendence? Rulla suggest three main factors that drive self-transcendence (pp.145-150).

The first, paradoxically relates to quite egocentric reasons. Here the ultimate goal is to achieve perfection through the realisation of one's own human potential. In that case the effort to reach the goal of self-transcendence is not to leave any potential of oneself unrealized. This is analogous to what Ignatius called the 'second man". This egocentric motivation, however, is too narrow and provides an insufficient reason for transcending the self.

The *second* possibility is what might be called a social-philanthropic motivation. The aim in this case is the desire to 'improve' humanity or society. This is a worthy goal but falls short of providing the needed motivation for any act of transcending the self that has ultimate meaning.

The *third* possible motive for self-transcendence relates to God – the search for the God who is truth, goodness and love without measure. Christians in general, and in particular those who have been chosen for the religious life or ordained ministry, aim to deepen the intimate relationship that God Himself has initiated by following Christ with a humble, obedient and pure heart.

Saint or sinner? Normal or pathological?

In daily life we easily assume that other people, and we ourselves, act consciously and deliberately at all times, This is shown, for example, in the way people assume that less attractive personal traits can be changed once we become aware of them. This way of thinking presupposes that people are internally free and conscious of the reasons for their behaviour. This common assumption about how human beings behave, easily leads to the conclusion that, with regard to candidates for ordination, all that is needed are good teachers and a competent Spiritual Director to enable them to learn, develop and grow in their calling.

If those who are responsible for the formation of future priests and deacons hold this view, they will expect students to be able to control their behaviour through prayer, increased knowledge, fraternal correction, and, if necessary, by being confronted. The assumption is that 'students, after being instructed, know what is required of them and that they, therefore, can change their behaviour when needed'.

A logical result of this way of thinking is that the behaviour of a candidate who does not abide by the rules or does not behave properly is judged solely by moral criteria. A candidate who does well enough and meets expectations is usually regarded as healthy, normal and virtuous. A candidate who acts in a way that is improper is considered either a problem or a sinner.

This approach, of course, completely ignores the extent to which human decisions and behaviour are influenced by unconscious forces. As described earlier, two extreme positions are commonly taken in relation to the interaction between the cognitive and the affective - intelligence and the free will on the one hand, and instincts and emotions on the other. So "two opposed exaggerations" may arise:

If one denies that the unconscious exists, and still more if one denies the possibility that it can have an active influence in the life of the healthy - as opposed to the pathological - person, then psychic life is assumed to be identical with conscious life. It follows that intelligence and will are thus given a privileged place.

Obviously, even proponents of such an exaggerated view must allow for the influence of instincts and emotions. But they hold, for example, that when there is a conflict between the disturbing influence of instinct or emotion and rational forces, the subject is nevertheless conscious of all the forces involved, both emotional and volitional. And equally, after the conflict is finished, the person concerned is said to be clearly capable of understanding whether emotion or will has prevailed, and if the act has been virtuous with reason dominating, or sinful in yielding to emotion. As Nuttin puts it so well: to this very day we are convinced in the depths of our heart that what happens within us is precisely as just described. In other words, one sees a man as a saint or a sinner, and life as facing the alternatives of virtue and vice. Now this is true, but it does not give a complete view of the person.

The opposite view that the unconscious is the *dominant* force in our psychic life is equally exaggerated. This is the thesis of classical psychoanalysis. In the conflict between rational and conscious forces on the one side, and unconscious emotional forces on the other, the unconscious forces are seen as acting in a secret and deceptive way. On this view, a person may mistakenly believe that they are making a conscious decision when in fact the agenda is being set by powerful unconscious drives which could be completely contrary to the conscious intention..

The first exaggeration tends to see the person in binary terms as either saint or sinner, a character of virtue or vice; the second tends to see the person as normal or pathological. It then follows that the daily limitations to which everyone is more or less subject will be grossly over-simplified and reduced to the categories of sin or pathological disorder (Rulla 80-81).

The problem with both viewpoints is that someone who does not conform to expectations, displays unacceptable behaviour, or is difficult to work with, is soon labelled as abnormal or sinful or simply written off as pathological. It then causes great confusion if any of these so-called 'fools' performs miracles or the nice friendly neighbour turns out to have committed heinous crimes. There are undoubtedly psychiatrists who would have diagnosed Teresa of Avila as hysterical and Jean Marie Vianney as a manic-depressive, while the Church canonized both of them. And who knows: perhaps both Church and psychiatrist might be right!

Rulla uses the term 'the first dimension' to describe that level of consciousness where a person is free to understand and accept responsibility for their moral behaviour. It is also at this level of consciousness that a person comes to choose the values which will be internalised through habituation.

Jumping ahead a bit, the third dimension in Rulla's theory is the unconscious level where the affective dynamics of instinct and emotion influence a person in ways the he himself may not understand. These unconscious forces can show themselves in the way ordinary feelings of jealousy can develop into a pathological jealousy that may even lead to murder. There is nothing wrong with a little bit of jealousy, especially in relation to a loved one, but extreme jealousy shows evidence of a more serious psychological problem.

In real life both these dimensions are simultaneously present in each one of us. The reason is that we are all driven by conscious and unconscious forces. The interface between the two is what

Rulla calls the 'second dimension'. It is at this level that instincts and emotions confront the 'spirit' - intelligence, reason and will. One of these may be able to push the other aside, in what von Weizsäcker calls 'the revolving door principle'. By this he means that 'if two psychic movements arise to awareness, one can drive out the other. For example, a decision can be cancelled or repressed by an unconscious drive, or a drive can be repressed by an act of will.' (cited in Rulla, p. 83). The issue is not whether this person lives consciously or unconsciously, but which of the two dimensions is dominant.

Research that we shall cite later has shown that this second level is dominant in most people. The first level dominates in a smaller percentage of people (the most mature). In a very small number of people the third level is dominant, and they tend to be very wounded or dysfunctional. Growth in holiness and spirituality may, in psychodynamic terms, be linked to growing maturity in the first dimension – that is to say, living more consciously at the cognitive level. This level of experience may even be called the trampoline, the preparatory phase for mystical experience.[54]

A person can be mentally healthy and a sinner at the same time. Somebody can be morally virtuous and also be psychologically unbalanced or even disturbed. The two conditions, in other words, can be found side by side in one person. The way a student will be seen and evaluated by members of the staff will depend strongly on the basic understanding of humanity held by the staff; if they think in terms of the of sinner-saint binary on the one hand and the healthy-sick category on the other, it is likely that only the external behaviour of the student will be taken into consideration.

---

[54] It is not possible to pursue this issue here in any depth. It deserves special consideration and study. The following is highly recommended: Evelyn Underhill, *Mysticism: a study in the nature and development of man's spiritual consciousness*, WPC 1955, reprinted by Meridian, Ontario, Canada, 1974. On p. 176 the author writes: 'First in the sequence of the mystic states, we must consider that decisive event, which is the awakening of the transcendental consciousness. This awakening, from the psychological point of view, appears to be an intense form of the phenomenon of 'conversion'; and closely akin to those deep and permanent conversions of the adult type which some religious psychologists call *sanctification*'. It is unnecessary to present all her conclusions on this subject; it is enough to point out that the matter has been given adequate treatment elsewhere. See also Evelyn Underhill, *Practical mysticism: a little book for normal people,* London, Dent & Sons, 1914.

If the candidate is good in terms of social and pastoral interaction, achieves good academic results, is obedient, leads a virtuous life and is observed praying in a devoted way, he is likely to be considered an ideal candidate for ordination. The assumption is that he lives predominantly in the first dimension. This kind of student invariably gets high marks and is rewarded with prizes and privileges, and is usually held up as an example to their peers. The question is seldom raised whether any of this is too good to be true. Experience has shown that these 'star pupils' will often fail to move into leading positions in their dioceses or congregations.

In fact, a surprising number of these 'ideal' candidates will actually become problems later and may eventually leave the ministry altogether, sometimes after they have caused a scandal. But were these not the exemplary candidates during training? What has been missed all along has been the influence of the third (unconscious) dimension. The exemplary behaviour of the candidate was not the product of cognitive ability and wholesome internalized values only, but sprang also from deeply rooted unconscious dynamics such as the need for approval, success or the fear of punishment and loss of affection.

At the same time, it is neither necessary nor healthy to become overly suspicious of aspirants - to screen each person with X-ray eyes and always be on the lookout for potential problems, as if most people are continually struggling in the third dimension. Quite a few saints have shown at times strange, perhaps even bizarre, patterns of behaviour, but they still lived mostly in the second or first dimension. It is only in cases of serious distortion, where the third dimension prevails disproportionately, that particular caution should be exercised.

A good psychological assessment will usually highlight any potential problem. The specialist who supervises the assessment should be someone, however, who is familiar with the realities of the spiritual life. Such a specialist should be sufficiently skilled to be able to discern whether an experience that appears to be a product of the third dimension might actually reflect elements of the first as well, and vice-versa. The question of hearing 'voices' or seeing apparitions would be a good example. It is a matter of careful assessment. All the forces at work in a person must be taken into account and seen as a whole, so that each person can grow to 'love the Lord your God with all your heart, and with all your soul, and with all your might' (Deut. 6, 5).

'Human formation, when it is carried out in the context of an anthropology which is open to the full truth of the human condition points towards completion in spiritual formation.'[55] Called to respond freely to the God who invites us to develop a relationship with Him, we are challenged to move beyond the obvious human limitations and rise above ourselves, towards self-transcendence. There is a constant tension between what we already are, and what we could and should become. This tension has a stronger influence on the processes of formation and holiness than we often realise.

Important dimensions of the unconscious

Since it is not possible within the scope of this chapter to give a systematic treatment of the unconscious, I want to limit myself to aspects of the unconscious (third dimension) that can play a significant role in the vocational process. Most people are not familiar with their own unconscious. While this is part and parcel of our human condition, there is a widespread fear of this dimension of life. We often find it easier to talk with somebody who has cancer or aids than with a person who is struggling with psychological problems. There is something about psychological disturbance that seems elusive, unknown, even uncanny. To be in touch with this inner part of the self requires an ability to overcome an instinctive fear.

Going on an interior journey is a bit like walking into a jungle. We enter a strange and fearsome world, full of frightening sounds and movements, a place which defies rational explanation. We have to spend some time in such a world to begin to feel at ease, to get to know the pathways and recognize the sounds, movements and rustlings. Only then will we discover the enormous possibilities that are hidden within this jungle - the beauty and the power as well as the very real danger. Gradually, that which initially inspired only fear begins to become more familiar as we get accustomed to it and are able to integrate it into our daily life.

---

[55] *Pastores Dabo Vobis*, 45.

It is never easy to get people to enter their own jungle. Resistance is often intense. Leaders in the faith community, those who have the responsibility of guiding individuals and communities, must make a priority, for the sake of loving others, of coming to know their inner selves. This is necessary if they are to avoid the inevitable pitfalls that will undermine their pastoral work or render it less effective. If they remain strangers to themselves, they may cause problems for the very people they want to help.

To require those who will be future leaders in the Church to engage in such a challenging self-examination is a matter of exercising 'tough love'. It is critically important that they should be required to work on these hidden inner forces for the sake of greater pastoral effectiveness as well as their own future, personal growth. What really matters is to achieve the degree of internal freedom that will enable candidates to make decisions and follow up on them without undue pressure from unconscious forces. Such a practice will help them gain expertise in the first dimension.

Growing in consistency

We speak of personal consistency when there is a healthy balance between instinctive or perceived needs, patterns of behaviour and declared spiritual values. When, for instance, someone claims that prayer is important, and he in fact feels the need to pray and does so regularly, we call him consistent. If he feels a need to pray in accordance with his professed values, but does not actually live a life of prayer, a consistent pattern is not yet psychologically or spiritually established.

Another example of psychological inconsistency would be the person who claims to want to forgive someone but nevertheless harbours strong feelings of revenge, and yet forgives the other person. If, however, his instinctive need for revenge overcomes the desire to forgive, we speak of social inconsistency.[56] A better balance will only be possible when he comes to understand what is driving the desire for revenge. This he can do by acquiring

---

[56] For further discussion, see Rulla, L., S.J., *Depth Psychology and Vocation: a Psycho-Social Perspective*, Gregorian University Press, Rome, 1990, pp. 82-88.

greater insight into his own dynamics. When that happens, the feelings of revenge will diminish and the ability to forgive will gain in strength. The Desert Fathers called this inner discernment process; 'Name the devil and he will disappear'.

Other examples of unconscious or hidden drives are dependency, aggression, autonomy, dominance, affirmation, exhibitionism, submission, excitement, sexual gratification, playfulness, need to be excited, desire for success, reactivity, change, humiliation, avoidance of criticism or pain, or even the need to care for others.[57] It is obvious that some of these hidden needs can make it particularly difficult to live a religious life, especially when unresolved personal issues exert their extraordinary power. Even so, none of this means that a person should be judged negatively on the basis of having such unresolved issues. What matters is that such issues are acknowledged and owned, that there is a clearer sense what to do with them, how to deal with them.

Every need has a positive and a negative pole. Some of these fit in well with the religious life and may actually strengthen it. Others can seriously distort relationships. But when we become aware of these powerful but hidden forces, we can gradually start to come to terms with them and use them for personal growth. Aggression, for example, can be a source of creativity, productivity and hope if it is harnessed productively. If it remains repressed, it will almost certainly lead to internal and external conflicts.[58] It is important to be clear: I am using the words 'value' and 'need' as Rulla defines them, that is 'values are innate tendencies to respond to objects as important in themselves while needs are innate tendencies related to objects as important for oneself' (p133).

---

[57] This list reflects transcultural values but is adapted to focus specifically on religious and priests. The list is based on the work of Murray, cited in Rulla, L.M., S.J., Ridick, J., S.S.C., Imoda, F., S.J., *Entering and Leaving Vocation: Intrapsychic Dynamics*, Gregorian University Press, Rome, 1988, pp. 352-353. See also a definition of *needs* in the same section.

[58] A more detailed treatment of feelings and emotions can be found in Manstead, A., Frijda, N., Fischer, A., (eds), *Feelings and Emotions; The Amsterdam Symposium*, Cambridge University Press, 2004. See also Arnold, M.B., *Feelings and Emotions; The Loyola Symposium*, Academic Press, New York, 1970.

Personal Conflicts

Research based on in-depth interviews, supplemented with various additional test results (Rorschach, Rotter, MMPI), has produced detailed data on 208 male and female religious, at the time of their entry into a community and again four years into training. The perceived degree of maturity of each person was plotted against a scale divided into four groups: all those who appeared to be under the influence of major internal conflict were placed in Group One (13.5% at entry), those assessed as nearly always influenced by inner conflict (46.5 % at entry) were placed in Group Two, those regularly influenced by inner conflict (28 % at entry) in Group Three, and everyone else who appeared only occasionally to be affected by major inner conflict (at entry 12 %) in Group Four.

A sequential study of the same group four years later put the percentages at 17%, 40.5% 28% and 14% respectively. For clarity, these results are set out below:

Active influence of Inner Conflict	At Entry to Religious Community	After four years
Group1: substantial	13.5%	17%
Group 2: intermediate	46.5%	40.5%
Group 3: regularly	28%	28%
Group 4: rarely	12%	14%

These data make clear that no significant growth in personal maturity occurred during those four years. Research among priests by Kennedy and Heckler in 1971 led to very similar results: poorly developed 8.5%; underdeveloped 66.5%; developing 18%; developed 7% (p145). Further, inner conflict for 86.5% of the candidates at entry was partially or wholly unacknowledged. Four years later this remained the case for 82.5 % of those interviewed.

The unavoidable conclusion is that personal psychodynamics are unlikely to change if left to the traditional priestly formation alone. Unless they are dealt with in a systematic and pro-active way, such unrecognized problems are likely to persist well after ordination. In the Kennedy and Heckler study, 79.5% of seminarians and 75% of active clergy fell into the first and second categories; 20.5% of new seminarians and 25% of the active clergy fell into the third and fourth categories.[59]

Working with Inner Conflict

Many people will find these figures deeply disturbing. Does this mean that the majority of religious are sick? Is not everyone allowed to have a few problems? Before jumping to conclusions, it is important to examine what is meant by 'inner conflict'. In the process of growing up, every person experiences a certain amount of normal inner tension or conflict when, for example, attempting to reach a particular goal. Tension by itself does not necessarily lead to frustration: we all recognise that some things take time. But there are tensions that are less benign. Healy gives the following example:

Imagine that I want to write an article. Once I have started, there is a normal concern to get on with it and finish the job. But after a while, I may begin to feel a certain amount of frustration because the article seems to be going nowhere. I cannot think clearly, still less get anything down on paper. I begin to feel perplexed. I persuade myself that it is only a question of time, of taking one step at a time. But then I begin to doubt myself. Would it not be better if I dropped the whole thing? This project is too much for me, it's beyond my capabilities.[60]

At this point, the inner tension has turned into a conflict between the wish to achieve a particular goal and the resistance that has reached the point of immobilizing me. I sense that this is no longer normal behaviour. I have to admit that there is a conflict going on within me that is revealing a struggle between the wish to complete the project and the presence of a sabotaging resistance. I know that I am perfectly capable of completing the article but I have reached the point where I feel sufficiently stuck to consider abandoning the project - even though I know that I possess the intellectual capacity to write a good article.

---

[59] Cf. *Entering and Leaving Vocation: intrapsychic dynamics*, pp. 144-145 A more in-detailed analysis is presented by the same authors in *Anthropology of the Christian Vocation: Vol. II Existential Confirmation*, Gregorian University Press, Rome, 1989.

[60] Healy, T., *The Challenge of Self-Transcendence*, p. 75.

This research data that were referred to earlier were based on the observed frequency of precisely this kind of regularly occurring conflict. The choice of a certain lifestyle necessitates agreeing to accept the values that go with that way of living. This means that one must accept the rules, customs, norms, and traditions that are a fundamental to the ethos of the profession, job or membership in an association that one has decided to join.

When it comes to wanting to become a priest, it demands the willingness to accept all the basic values of Christian discipleship, in common with every follower of Christ. But ordination also calls for the commitment to poverty, obedience, and chastity that the Church requires of her priests. Those who say that they want to become a priest are choosing to live by values which are part and parcel of the ordained vocation – values such as being committed to a strong prayer practice, acquiring pastoral skills, practicing celibacy, charity, obedience, forgiveness, living a simple life, exercising healthy leadership, and working together with others.

Conflicts can be engendered or discovered during formation and training but can also come to light following ordination. It is, therefore, the responsibility of a seminary or institute for theological education to structure its formation in such a way that students' inner conflicts can surface, become apparent and be worked through.

It is the task of a formation program to enable inner conflicts to surface so that candidates can begin to learn to deal with them in a healthier and mature manner. Since inner conflicts vary greatly from person to person, the formation process needs to be tailored to meet the psychological dynamics of the individual. It is especially urgent to prevent such unsolved inner conflicts from emerging after ordination. Problems in the parish, whether old or new, frequently trigger such inner conflicts in the newly ordained priest or deacon.

Many painful experiences of extreme loneliness, burnout, depression, unbearable stress, irrational competitiveness, and authoritarian behaviour can be prevented if the unresolved factors that have contributed to these issues are forced to the surface during the years of formation. This is critically important if the damage caused in parish ministry by clergy with such unacknowledged inner conflicts is to be avoided.

Training Institutes that are satisfied and even proud of the fact that the majority of their students pass through training without facing any personal crises are in danger of abandoning their responsibility to help candidates understand themselves better. They are also probably neglecting their duty to the Church.

The clergy who graduate from such a seminary are unlikely to have grown in self-understanding to any significant degree. The study mentioned before has shown that 82.5% of interviewees still had not engaged with their inner troubled dynamics after four years of ministry. Those responsible for formation, therefore, need to have enough insight and knowledge of the candidate to gain a sense of the personal issues that need to be worked on, both in terms of how often they may manifest themselves and how serious they may be. It is also, of course, important to judge the degree of positive motivation and committed faith so that these factors can be taken into consideration when such issues or conflicts become apparent later on.

Another question that needs to be faced during the admission process is which model of training is right for each particular candidate. Even then, other practical questions are equally important: the model may be right, but does the institute possess the necessary knowledge and skills to be able to guide this candidate effectively?

It is not enough that candidates are required to go through an initial process of psychological screening. These tests are not designed to yield the necessary data on the issues identified above. Furthermore, many of the agencies involved in this initial screening may fail to recognise potential problems. For example in terms of human sexuality, patterns of behaviour reported by candidates may appear perfectly normal to secular psychologists when in fact they would be utterly inappropriate in a religious vocation. The psychologist may also consider it absurd for an adult man to promise obedience to a bishop, and consider any signs of inner resistance to such a requirement perfectly healthy.

Training institutions have the right to set high expectations for their graduates provided they themselves are applying equally high standards to their own work in supporting and encouraging students to grow in self-understanding. They can, of course, opt to lower the bar. No doubt that would make life a lot easier both for students and the faculty.

If that choice is made everything may appear to be peaceful and everybody content with many appreciative smiles all round. But the consequence is that inner conflict remains unacknowledged; it will continue to lurk beneath the surface ready to burst out later, most likely after ordination. Experience shows that few are ready to accept responsibility for their own inner turmoil. Most will blame some predicament or some person and try to manipulate the situation to cope with their feelings of tension. Pastoral teams and parishioners thus pay a high price for the neglect of these issues during training.

The newly ordained pastor may displace his inner turmoil by engaging in inappropriate activity outside the parish – activities that may well betray the values he claims to hold dear. Displacement or projection onto others may allow the priest to live with himself for a while. He may appear to be cultivating an atmosphere of 'mutual respect' in an environment of 'live and let live'. But all the time, the tension is building up as the priest plays off the pastoral team and the parish to deal with his own problems - just the opposite of the way things should be in a ministry of pastoral care and service. A collusive pattern can develop which creates a culture where accommodations are made in order to avoid confronting the issues.

This is the challenge both for the training institute and, of course, for the candidate himself. Can they meet the demands of facing up to the actuality of a person's inner turmoil? Indeed, is this demanding and sometimes gruelling process of personal formation even feasible in the case of older candidates who are used to leading their own lives, holding established and often responsible roles in the community, and often occupying a high professional status? At the end of the day, it is the candidate's life, the candidate's mission, the candidate's future, and the candidate's vocation and therefore it might be expected that the candidate himself is the first interested in resolving conflicts.

It is in the interests of both the candidate and the Church to acknowledge the psychological reality of inner unresolved conflicts. It is difficult, and often people have to be helped and encouraged to cross the threshold and begin this journey of inner exploration. Experience shows that most candidates are sensible and happy enough to accept help once it is offered. But, in their own interest, a few sometimes have to be challenged.

I am aware that the approach I am advocating may seem a bit negative, pessimistic, even oppressive. From my point of view, however, this way of confronting and dealing with personal issues during formation is pragmatic, based on realism. Research and practical experience both suggest that there are too many painful and complex pastoral situations which have arisen because inner conflict has been ignored or denied.

Pastoral problems arise normally not because of lack of faith or a lack of practical training as such. They arise rather from pre-existing psychological dynamics of the candidate before he is accepted for training.

The Dynamic Self

The inner struggle between competing needs can take place at several different levels. In his book *Entering and Leaving Vocation* (pp. 9-15) Rulla describes the different dynamic components of the underlying sense of the *self*. The *self* in fact consists of two basic components - the *Ideal Self* (IS) and the *Real Self* (RS). The first one, the IS, also has two levels which he calls the *Ideal Institutional Self* (IIS) and the *Ideal Personal Self* (IPS). The first of these, the IIS, is what the person thinks the institution - the Church, the diocese - expects of him. Not, in other words, what the Church's expectations are, but what the person thinks the Church expects from him. The *Ideal Personal Self* (IPS) refers to what the priest personally holds to be a core value as well as his image of what he would like to be or do.

The *Real Self* (RS) is also multi-layered and consists of the *Manifest Self* (MS) and the *Latent Self* (LS). The MS is what the person consciously knows himself to be. The LS is made up of character traits of which the priest is not aware, such as needs and emotions which lie beneath the surface of conscious thought but can be partially accessed through projective tests. This *Latent Self* is actually an integral part of the Real Self. Imoda suggests that this unconscious part of the LS contains an area which is reserved for Mystery. This mystery can never be fully comprehended by human thought, nor should attempts be made to accomplish what is beyond human reach.[61]

---

[61] Imoda, F., S.J, *Human Development: Psychology and Mystery*, Peeters, 1998, Louvain, Studies in Spirituality, supplement 2, translation of *Sviluppo*

Some inner struggles, such as the tension which regularly arises between the Ideal Personal Self and the Ideal Institutional Self, are not difficult to understand. As a routine part of the admissions processss, for example, we often inquire about the faith of the aspirant, his view of the Church, his image of God, and his expectations of the priesthood. In this way we are in fact constructing a picture of his Ideal Personal Self. When we ask what he thinks that the Church expects of him as a priest, he is likely to display his Ideal Institutional Self (IIS).

Asking him what he thinks about priests is one thing, asking what he thinks the Church expects of priests is something else altogether. For example, one candidate might be aware of the acute shortage of priests and be tempted to think that he can pick and choose the kind of priestly ministry that he finds congenial. . This kind of response shows that he has little idea of what *incardination* means, especially in relation to obedience to the Bishop who could well appoint him to a completely different type of ministry or parish, way outside his comfort zone.

Other candidates may have hopelessly unrealistic 'heroic' notions of sacrificial ministry in which they gallantly put aside their own aspirations and see the priest as a puppet in the hands of the bishop or superior. Others aspirants or students are more Roman Catholic than the Pope and fantasize about pre-conciliar notions of the priesthood.

First-year students who have read official Church documents on the priesthood or the diaconate are often shocked when they begin to grasp the Church's view of priesthood and what she expects of her priests. For some these expectations are more stringent than they expected. Others find that they are not as bad as they feared. And some discover what they expected all along and have no trouble accepting what the Church requires of them.

These internal struggles between the IPS and the IIS tend to be fairly obvious and relatively easy to talk about, interpret or explain. Such a clarification of tensions between the IPS and the IIS also makes it less difficult for the student to come to a decision. They are at any rate easier to bring to the surface than those conflicts that involved unconscious factors.

Umano Psicologia e Mistero.

Motivation

Motivation plays a critically important role in conflict, as was made clear by Healy's example of the man who cannot finish writing an article, even though he is fully capable of doing so. His Ideal Self, so to speak, wants to write the article, but unconscious forces are at work in the Real (Latent) Self hold him back. As the realisation gradually dawns that the real situation is significantly more complicated, it would be all too easy to say something like 'that is too bad' and leave it at that.

But here is a person who is unable to achieve something that is well within his capabilities. He is aware that something is holding him back, something that has to do with his development is tying him down but he does not understand why this is happening. If he abandons the project there will be at least two losses. The first is that the author fails to achieve his full potential, and the second one is that others will not benefit from his potential insight.

The psychological drivers that shape his action, or rather his inaction, consist of dynamic forces that are outside his control and it is precisely these forces which steer him towards an outcome obviously contrary to his conscious desire. Unless these subconscious issues are addressed, this struggle can continue to frustrate such a person throughout their lifetime. They can also profoundly affect his relationships not only with other people but with God. It can feel as if there are two horses pulling the person in two different directions at the same time. One pulls towards the Divine to deepen his relationship with God (his conscious desire) while the other, simultaneously, pulls in exactly the opposite direction (the unconscious motivation).

Nobody wants to look a fool and, therefore, such a person will routinely come up with all sorts of excuses. He is unable to admit that he cannot do it, and will find excuses like not having the time, or no longer being interested. Such a candidate knows that he is not really speaking the truth but settles for fiction because he can see no other way out. What he needs to do, of course, is harness the two horses more effectively so they start pulling in the same direction. This means first and foremost having the courage to face up to the existence of unconscious forces and start to bring them to the surface where they can be understood, worked through and dealt with.

Many instances of such unresolved inner conflicts can be given from the actual practice of ministry, both before and after ordination. Let me give a few brief examples:

- A priest enters church for Mass and sees only a handful of people in the congregation. He feels angry, even though he understands that at the *ideal* level, numbers do not make any difference: worship is worship. So why does he feel so angry? He is mature enough to recognize that the anger he feels is way out of proportion to the actual situation. He decides to seek help to explore his emotional reaction a little more.

  He arranges to meet up with a counsellor, and after a few interviews he starts to recognise that he has a deep-seated 'need to be needed'. He also begins to see how this need has in fact always been an important element in his motivation to become a priest. He sees that he is dependent on the recognition he receives from others – the congregation, those who call on him as a pastor, and so on. But he also starts to realize how much this 'need to be needed' restricts his inner freedom and constrains his pastoral ministry.

- A student who gets along reasonably well with the Rector and appreciates his qualities, nevertheless sharply and unkindly criticizes the man on a regular basis. This pattern of behaviour is pointed out to him, but he is at a loss to explain why he behaves in this way. The same pattern continues after ordination, except this time it is not the Rector who is on the receiving end of his sharp tongue, but the bishop or the chairman of the parish council. It inevitably places a strain on relationships, the exact opposite of what he wants to achieve. He wants help, but he is held back by some inner resistance.

  Eventually, things get to the point where he gives in and starts to explore these inner dynamics that are causing these conflicts. Slowly, he starts to understand that he sees anyone in authority as a replica of his father, who used to punish him severely for any kind of minor misdemeanour. As a child, he lived in constant anxiety of provoking his father, for fear of even greater the punishment.

Once he begins to understand this process of projection and transference, he is able to work on the ingrained pattern of his behaviour. Relationships with others begin to improve, particularly with those in authority. He comes to see them as they are, and react, no longer as the frightened schoolboy he had been, but as a mature person. The likelihood is that his relationship with God also becomes more mature at much the same time.

- Quite a few people complain of being distracted in prayer, especially during meditation. They have tried all the traditional means of spiritual discipline, they get tired of their own failures, and may even begin to wonder if they really love God. When asked to describe carefully what actually happens during times of silence, the most varied answers are given.

  One person described a kind of phantom standing behind and watching him. Another tells of being distracted by all the things he still had to do that day. A third is only aware of anxiety. For years they have tried to do all 'the right things' – they have followed the familiar advice to 'keep going', as in 'name the distraction and then consciously bring yourself back to prayer' and so on. But it seldom seems to work. In the end they give up, and settle for reading a spiritual book instead.

Patient reflection with a suitably qualified mentor or counsellor will help the one who is haunted by a phantom to recognize, for example, the mother, now dead, who had once continually demanded (too much) attention. Or help the one who is distracted by responsibilities to become aware of feelings of guilt about tasks left unfinished in the past. Or help the one who is plagued by anxiety to discern heretofore unacknowledged guilt or shame about feelings of aggression he cannot accept.

By being able to name dynamics which have operated below the surface of awareness, the real problems can be dealt with. By allowing these inner repressed feelings, these 'little devils', to come to the surface of awareness, each candidate can gradually start to deal with the real problem. In doing this, the way is opened to experiencing silent prayer without so much hindrance. It is almost as if God is using the conflicted feelings experienced in prayer to urge spiritual growth by being more in touch with recognizing more of the truth. Spirituality and psychology go hand in hand in the life of prayer. The way of relating to God is not different than the way the individual relates to others.

Many people regard themselves as 'perfectionists' – it sounds good, and conveys a strong sense of responsibility. The problem is that perfectionists look at everything as a job to be done well, even going on vacation. So leisure becomes another assignment. Everything has to be meticulously planned, nothing is allowed to go wrong, everything must be done on time, and even getting perfect grades is not enough.

For 'perfectionist' clergy, liturgy needs to be done faultlessly. They are tired of themselves, they become aware that they are running ahead of themselves in a state of near exhaustion, but they excuse their behaviour with 'That's the way I am, I'm a perfectionist.' Meanwhile they are driving others who are forced to go along with their perfectionism up the wall. When something *does* go wrong, they may become utterly distraught, sometimes to the point of becoming depressed. 'What do you mean fatigued?', they say. 'Stressed? Burned out? I'm immune to such things'. Or so they think.

It sometimes helps to ask such people what they believe would happen if they gave up this anxious search for perfection. Often, they cannot even imagine what life would be like in such a circumstance. The drive is too ingrained. Nevertheless, the exercise can help them sometimes to see what really lies behind this persistent and utterly unrealistic drive for perfection: fear of being blamed, fear of being criticized, fear of guilt feelings, fear of failure. For them guilt means punishment, and that means the kind of rejection that is intolerable. This in turn may activate aggressive feelings because something in their unconscious screams 'I am not guilty!'

The vicious circle is thus completed, because the perfect priest can never allow himself to be angry, so they do not feel anger either. At least, that is what the priest insists. The perfectionist is so anxious to avoid all such feelings that there is no possibility of admitting them consciously. Another example of a similar mechanism would be the candidate who is so driven by guilt over some perceived failure to care that they see a vocation to the priesthood as a way of demonstrating their commitment to 'doing good'. The candidate himself, or course, is highly unlikely to admit that this is the case.

Most of us are familiar with authoritarian personalities. They are usually dogmatic, assertive and demanding. The psychological dynamics behind this condition are complex, but a frequent factor is a fear that manifests itself in a variety of camouflaged ways.

What about priests who are faithful in prayer when they are with others but as soon they are away on holiday do not even bother to pray. The obvious question is to what extent this person has really internalized a life of prayer? Does such a person only conform in order to be accepted by their community? Regular praying at any rate has not yet become a personally meaningful habit.

What about the priest who feels compelled to visit the same family twice a week and stays till 11:00 pm because 'they need me so much'. It would be more honest to ask 'who needs whom?' That priest may need to take a long hard look in the mirror before he discovers that he is more likely to be afraid of being alone. Better to admit this and to have a chance to deal with his fear more honestly.

Or there is the student who *must* get high grades all the time. He is furious and unhappy with himself when his marks are not as good as they 'ought' to be. Why the anger? Could it be that he has not learned to accept the normal limitations of being human? The truth is that even something as laudable as serious academic study can become yet another defence mechanism to stave off fear and guilt. Knowledge is power and it allows the person to feel independent and in control.

Who knows, maybe someone higher up will be impressed by him and consider him for promotion. On the surface the presented motive for ordination is the highly laudable desire to serve the Church and unselfishly use the talents the Lord has given him. Sometimes the reason given for working hard is 'I just like studying' or 'I like being under pressure'. Such a candidate rarely has the detachment needed to stand back and see how much he is driven by the unconscious desire to be noticed.

There are other students who are almost impossible to motivate. Generally they are open and friendly but after a while they start to irritate people. It is often difficult to understand why this is so.

They procrastinate, dither, are always late, and forgetful. But they are invariably pleasant and apologetic. The result is that few dare to confront them. Their behaviour is explained away with 'that's the way they are'. Such students can have a paralyzing effect on the team to which they have been assigned. They would like to be different. They do not understand why they always put things off until the last possible moment, even if they had plenty of time to plan ahead and get things done.

Their behaviour is frequently put down to poor time management. Such students may even take courses aimed at helping them change their procrastinating habits. But these rarely work. Sooner or later they will slip back into the same old pattern. If they are persuaded to start exploring the latent psychological dynamics shaping their behaviour, they may start to see that this procrastination is nearly always a way of dealing with unrecognised dissatisfaction or aggression.

They will probably deny this at first – sometimes vehemently - but with patience and support they may come to recognize and accept what is really going on within themselves. Only then will they be in a position to deal with the latent anger and the frustration they have been unable to handle in any other way. It may take a lot of patience to get such students to the point of admitting their anger. Once they have faced up it, however, they are more likely to learn new ways of coping in a more adult way.

These are just a few examples of unresolved inner conflicts in candidates for ministry that often occur and are relatively straightforward. Volumes could be written about some of the more complex conditions that I have encountered. I am thinking, for example, of inner struggles about the nature of God, sin and guilt, unresolved affective-sexual conflicts, or competition for power in pastoral teams, not to mention cases involving abuse and addiction. The list would become very lengthy indeed.

The important thing to grasp is that inner conflicts are part of the normal human condition. The issue is not *always* one of being emotionally or psychically disturbed. Everybody has conflicting, unconscious emotions. Only God is absolutely free. The important question is to what extent does inner turmoil adversely affect my personal life and my pastoral work? Everyone can blow a fuse now and then, but when the lights go off every day there is something wrong that needs attention. This does *not* have to mean being excluded from the priesthood, even if one's unresolved conflicts are rather severe. It does mean using the time in formation to grow in self-awareness and understanding, to deal and resolve these conflicted feelings as fully as possible.

Inner conflict only becomes a problem when the pastor allows them to dominate his ministry and thus undermine his pastoral relationships. Candidates who fall into what has been described earlier as Categories II and III (those experiencing major or regular inner conflict) do require special care, right from the start of training. Productive and careful work with such candidates is often a slow process and success is never guaranteed. This means that every centre engaged in priestly formation needs to have someone on its faculty with the necessary skills to accompany all the candidates.

The training and formation of pastoral workers, older as well as younger ones, is thus an intensive process which demands a structured and planned approach, as well as the support of professional people of various disciplines. It just will not do to accept someone only on the basis of strong faith and perceived good nature. Our world is growing more and more complicated. Individuals and their life experience are also becoming more varied and complex. Ministers these days are exposed to more and more stressful situations. Increasingly pastoral work takes place in pastoral teams where clergy and laity must work together. It takes a lot of goodwill and hard work to take everyone seriously and give them the opportunity to develop into the kind of priest who is able to answer the pastoral needs of diverse communities, to be a blessing to others, and to learn to flourish as a priest as well.

Psychospiritual integration is a shared journey

The approach to the formation of candidates for ordination just outlined could be threatening to some. To keep spirituality and psychology firmly separated seems easier and safer. The influence of the 'self-fulfilment philosophy' of the 1960s and 70s has been enormous, not least in the Church and its educational practices. The Church, unfortunately, has not done enough in the years since then to train the specialists needed to ensure that the human sciences are taken seriously in the process of formation.

The unhappy result of this oversight is twofold. First, it is now very difficult to find competent people who are qualified in both spirituality and psychology and, second, those in authority do not quite know what to do with problem cases in the pastorate. The downside of this situation is that candidates or students are only referred for psychotherapy when they have obvious and serious problems. Often there is no room in the regular curriculum for diagnosis, preventive care and processing of internal conflicts.

It is true that today most dioceses and religious orders expect aspirants to go through a process of psychological screening before they are accepted into training. However, existing procedures are in many cases seriously inadequate. There is, first of all, the issue of professional confidentiality which severely limits what the psychologist can put down on paper. As a result the carefully guarded language that is typically employed is often of limited use to those responsible for the student.

A second problem is that secular psychological methods are not designed to discern the internal degree of freedom that is needed for a person to live according to Gospel values. The standard psychological tests only aim to describe general character traits and to measure a person's capacity for academic study and professional development. Further, because the candidate knows that the tests will be used to assess his suitability for training he will often try, either consciously or unconsciously, to manipulate the process in order to achieve a favourable outcome - even though it is possible to detect such manipulation.

On a number of occasions I have been asked to test candidates for other religious institutions. Sometimes, I have been left with the suspicion that the process was driven more by a negative concern within the institution to avoid 'problem cases' than a positive concern to establish a good psychological basis for the candidate's further development. Unless it is decided to require *every* candidate in the entire country to take a pre-enrolment screening test, I am not in favour of such tests when they are used only *at the time of admission* to decide on a candidate's suitability for ordination.

At Bovendonk, it was a requirement that every potential student must be prepared to undertake a psychological assessment if the staff feel that this is advisable. As far as initial contact with candidates is concerned, I prefer a common sense approach that uses ordinary human capacities for observation to make an informed assessment. All that is required at this stage is to ascertain that the student is capable of growth in self-understanding. Initial conversations are simply intended to lay out the preliminary foundations for this important work. Only when a shared commitment to constructive growth has been established is it appropriate to consider more formal psychological tests. The aim of these initial conversations is to make candidates interested and motivated to discover more about themselves.

To accomplish this, it can be very useful and sometimes necessary during the admissions process and during his training, to raise stress to the optimum level that a particular candidate can tolerate at this point in his life, simply to help him become aware of the conflicts that need to be worked through for the sake of his future vocation as priest or deacon. Naturally, this requires the presence of faculty members who are capable of helping students deal with the issues that presented themselves during the intake process or after, whether or not these were intentionally provoked.

Our experience has been that this is done most effectively if each student is allocated a special mentor during the first two years of training. In the overwhelmingly male environment of the seminary, it is preferable that the mentoring is done by qualified women. They are usually better at seeing what is really going on in such circumstances.

As an aside, it is extraordinary how few church workers will take the initiative to seek professional help with their own issues of growth and development. Rather than seek help and support crisis on, most seem to prefer to let things come to a point of point where Church authorities have to intervene.

Integrating spirituality and psychology

Some will judge that this approach contains far too much psychology. All that is necessary, they may say, is a good Spiritual Director. Unfortunately, experience has confirmed that this is not true. I am convinced though that there were no better psychologists in the past than, for instance, the Desert Fathers and the great saints of old. Of course there still are Spiritual Directors in our time who are able to accomplish very much with a candidate, and also come to mean much to him, by employing only the language of spirituality.

On the other hand, so many complex inner dynamics can be at play that often another method, another approach, with skills that are complimentary, is required to reach deep lying conflicts that are also a normal part of the human condition. I often compare this to the relationship between a patient and his dentist. If we are smart we regularly visit our local dentist. However, while maintaining overall responsibility for our treatment and on-going dental care, the dentist may refer us, when needed, for special treatment to an oral surgeon.

So it is also with spiritual formation. We need a Spiritual Director, but the director may occasionally need to refer us to a specialist in human dynamics who can help use deal with particular issues or problems that have arisen. Our Spiritual Director remains in overall control, but simply draws, when needed, on the skills of appropriate specialist help. A specialist can help us explore difficult issues in a supportive and professional environment. This can lead to discoveries about the self that can then, with the help of our Spiritual Director, be integrated into our life of faith.

It sometimes happens that a candidate seeks professional help on his own initiative, but is then told by his Spiritual Director that such help is stuff and nonsense. This is a recipe for disaster! To give but one example, a particular candidate continues to feel a profound sense of guilt that is way out of proportion to any reasonable understanding of sin despite regular visits to a Spiritual Director, frequent reception of the sacraments, faithful review and confession. It is almost certain that in such a situation the cause is a chronic, unresolved inner conflict. When that happens, spiritual direction seems to be going nowhere and the Spiritual Director is reduced to pointing this out over and over.

Common sense would suggest that another approach might help this candidate explore the reasons for the underlying conflict. A qualified, objective outsider could help the candidate to uncover the guilt feelings that underlie the conflict. Is this so ridiculous or far-fetched? These problems are very common and occur frequently right across the spectrum of backgrounds and experiences. They are also statistically normal.

The only people not likely to experience such problems are those defined by the research project to be among 12 to 14% in Group

IV. Those belonging to this minority are seldom swayed by inner conflict. If problems do arise, they know how to deal with them, either by themselves or with some advice from others. People in this group are much easier to mentor. The truth, however, is that most Church workers do not fall into this category.

The conversation between theology and the human sciences is in its infancy. Interdisciplinary research is beginning to happen at the academic level[62], but in the actual practice of educating men for Holy Orders much is left undone, despite repeated appeals from the *Magisterium* to make more use of the human sciences.

---

[62] See, for example: Browning, D.S., *Can Psychology escape Religion?* And, Forte, B., *Theology and Psychology*, in: Imoda, F., S.J., *A Journey to Freedom*, Peeters, Leuven, 2000. Studies in Spirituality supplement 5, particularly chapters 2 and 3.

8. LEARNING FROM EXPERIENCE

By Matt Ham

> *When I was a child, I spoke like a child,*
> *I thought like a child, I reasoned like a child;*
> *when I became a man,*
> *I gave up childish ways.*
> (I Cor. 13, 11)

> *Truly I say to you, unless you turn*
> *and become like children,*
> *you will never enter the kingdom of heaven.*
> (Mt. 18,3)

Introduction

These two apparently contradictory texts with which Imoda opens his book *Human Development Psychology and Mystery*[63] speak to the personal experience of adult men who hold down a job and at the same time follow a part-time training programme for the priesthood or diaconate. Seventy-eight men have been ordained over these past twenty-four years through our part-time course. Their average age at ordination was 43, which means an average of age 37 when they started their training.

All of them had finished school many years before, completed their professional training, and had either been employed for some time or lived in a religious community. In other words, their personalities had been formed, they had built up a body of knowledge and experience, and they knew what life was about. They had been independent and carried professional responsibility, perhaps even owned their businesses. They had been members of a faith community in which they had played an active role and where they built up an understanding of the Church and its different ministries.

---

[63] Imoda, F., S.J., *Sviluppo Umano, Psicologia e Mistero*, Ed. Piemme, 1993. English translation available in: *Studies in Spirituality,* supplement 2, Peeters, Leuven, 1998.

Last but not least, most candidates for the diaconate are also married. They know what married life is about and are often parents. A few were widowers. Some had responsibility for the education of their children, with all the satisfactions and the cares associated with that. In short, we are talking of mature men, established in life, people who are used to standing on their own two feet, and making up their own minds.

They not only have an understanding of the world, but also an image of God, and all of this has helped to shape their own patterns of behaviour. Then they ask to train for the priesthood or diaconate while they continue in their trade or profession – as a carpenter or builder, engineer, government official, funeral director, lawyer, nurse, teacher, baker, salesman, town councillor or whatever.

It is a daunting challenge, and one can understand why established seminaries hesitate to accept this kind of mature candidates. Can adults change? Will adults be able to commit themselves unreservedly to the Church? The first question that arises is if it really is necessary to change that much? And, what is meant by 'change' anyway? The second question has to do with to whom and what, aside from God, they must commit themselves to?

Those who assume that older students will resist being drilled or straitjacketed are right. Older candidates are not inclined to accept what is simply poured out over them. Why should they? On the other hand candidates who think they can simply 'do their own thing' in formation and thereafter have to learn that this is not acceptable either. And if some think they can continue to live their lives as they were used to doing, then they are also wrong and sooner or later someone is going to have to tell them.

There also are many misunderstandings about the concept of part-time training. There are fewer suspicions than in the past, but they have not disappeared completely. Can a part-time programme turn out good priests? Is it really possible to have a second chance, a second career? Part-time sounds like second best to some people, like lowering the bar and debasing the currency, even though experience proves otherwise.

On the other hand, there are also candidates who think that part-time formation is less demanding, that they can skip through without any serious effort or radical change. Some may opt for part-time, rather than full-time residential training under the illusion they will be able to absorb the new without having to give up the old. Such candidates will quickly discover during their first year that this is not quite the way it works. If not, they will not last.

When an adult returns to study and discovers that there is still a lot to learn, not only on an intellectual level, but also in practical pastoral matters, he will often report a sense of being infantilized. As a former student in his fifties once told me after he had done a few months of pastoral training: 'I used to make decisions about people, about large amounts of money, but now I feel as if I have two left hands. I am like a child!'

Candidates have to give up a lot to become priests: valuable possessions, a drop in income, loss of status, being criticized by one's family, or perhaps even losing friends. Then on top of it all, they may be required to drop familiar ways and learn new ways. This list is not produced simply for dramatic effect, or to arouse sympathy for the candidate. On the contrary, the list of demands and changes required simply illustrates the degree of commitment required from those mature students who feel called to ordained ministry in later life.

This is no easy option: just look at the number of candidates who complete the course: 60% instead of 50% in seminaries for younger people – that is 10% higher. I have often been told that it is precisely this strong determination and commitment that impresses so many of our lecturers and mentors and persuades them to give up their week-ends to help with the training. When the students begin to realize how much their lecturers are giving in order to help them, the relationship between them becomes a reciprocal one and the students are strengthened in their own commitment.

Nevertheless, older students are often confronted with deeper concerns than mere intellectual demands or practical matters. They are often required to face up to some of their own unresolved psychological or pastoral needs. Their own inner motivation has to be explored and taken right back to its spiritual root. Vocation is a matter of being touched by God; but this is itself something which is difficult to articulate for it concerns a personal religious experience which can take on very different forms.

But whatever form it takes, this encounter with God will necessarily move them in a new direction or deepen something that has probably been dormant for a long time. Every vocation must be understood and assessed from a theological and spiritual perspective. This is a process that, once begun, is likely to take them farther than they imagined possible when they first started. Give God an inch and He will often take a mile; one chink in the armour may allow the grace of God to take over your whole being. Daily prayer, frequent reception of the sacraments, spiritual reading, spiritual direction, retreats and Quiet Days, the study of Holy Scripture, Church history, philosophy, theology and the human sciences, all contribute to more insight into the meaning of ordained ministry to which the candidate feels so profoundly called.

But many other things are also likely to be questioned. How do you regard the world and what is your own place within it? How do you relate to other people? What do you think about the Church and how do you stand within that community? What is it that drives your inner life and motivation? In the end, no aspect of your life is sacrosanct, no string left untouched. This is what it means to choose a new way of life. It is more than simply changing your job in order to earn a better living. If you think that a priest can have two lives, keeping priestly ministry carefully sealed away from everything else, then you are wrong. Priesthood embraces the whole person. This is what the Church expects and teaches through the *Magisterium.* It is what is expected of all candidates for ordained ministry.

Across the whole world there are significant differences in the way seminaries emphasize various aspects of training for priesthood. Each institute stresses a distinctive aspect of formation. In India, for example, there is an increasing tendency to integrate parts of Indian eastern spirituality into Christian faith and priestly ministry. I know from my own experience that the emphasis in Brazil has been for decades on the theology of liberation, which has certainly had an impact on the life training of priests.

In the Netherlands and Belgium there are also differences in emphasis between the dioceses which are reflected in the seminaries they use and support. Inevitably, one hears talk about progressive, liberal, conservative, or dogmatic approaches, and all shades in between. Without denying, however, that there are real differences of emphasis, I am nevertheless convinced that all the institutes responsible in the Netherlands for priestly formation basically strive to prepare their candidates for the same universal Catholic priesthood.

Perhaps it is easy in practice for the training agenda to be dominated by the practical problems faced by priests in contemporary ministry and lose sight of the overall theological framework and vision of ministry. Religious orders and congregations have their Constitutions and Rules which shape the pattern of training they adopt. This limits the degree of personal influence of those with oversight in these communities can exercise when compared with diocesan institutions. But apart from sacred scripture and official Church documents and policy statements, diocesan institutes have little to go on other than the traditions of their diocese and the memories the staff have of their own formation. This means that there is always a danger that the shape and content of the training programme will simply reflect the subjective preferences of the Rector and his staff.

In terms of academic requirements, the situation is radically different – the details of the syllabus are very precisely prescribed. But for the rest, there are endless reports and reviews which make countless recommendations on the criteria for the selection of candidates and on pastoral aspects of formation. The same applies to spiritual formation of the diocesan priest; in my opinion only a few diocesan institutes have really come to grips with this aspect of priestly formation. Within this framework, there is plenty of room for diversity. The moment we touch on questions of personality and self-understanding, however, the directives and criteria become vague and seldom go beyond broad generalities.

And it is precisely this deeper personal dimension which sooner or later will come to the surface in training. If we ask parishioners or diocesan staff officers what are the most common problems faced by them in relation to priests, the answer is seldom liturgy or preaching, pastoral visiting, prayer or other pastoral matters. The most common complaints are about communications, team work, management, negative attitudes towards outsiders, leading a double life, inflexibility, authoritarian behaviour, absence at workshops and so on. We hear about aggressive defensiveness, unreasonable demands for better living conditions, showing off and attention-grabbing, or inflated long-windedness which avoids the real issues.

If on the other hand we listen to the complaints of priests, we hear a quite different story: we hear about loneliness, overwork, crowded agendas, interference and diocesan bureaucrats, demanding or difficult parishioners, lack of faith (by other people of course), and living in a modern society where religion is more or less marginalized. If you then add to the list those aspects of a priest's private life which are not placed in the open by either side, you get a sense of the negative if not destructive picture of clergy which seems to be so common. It is enough to make anyone depressed. When I discuss these things with first year students, they ask if I am trying to scare them into dropping out because, they tell me, I am close to succeeding.

It is not my intention to examine in detail the reality of any of these complaints against the clergy. In fact, I am convinced that the vast majority of priests search for God through an honest commitment to Christ. They are dedicated to their parish work, and most people most of the time appreciate and like them. They are unselfish and give themselves entirely to their ministry. They live a life of prayer and do their best to deepen their faith by all available means. They do not make the headlines because there is nothing sensational about them. Having said all that, they are adults and do not need of my protection. All I want to say is that most of the common complaints made about priests have little or nothing to do with faith or the broader Church. They are the problems of normal human relationships and priests suffer from them just the same as anyone else. The problems of personality may be obvious or they may be hidden; but either way they are there, long before ordination.

For example, someone who from early on has been anxious, unsure of himself, on the defensive, scrupulous (i.e. suffering of disproportionate guilt feelings), inflexible, or a combination of all of these things will most likely be inclined later to appeal to external sources of authority or laws (even divine law!), to persuade other people, or to retain control over them. Another who does not have these characteristics will not succumb to such temptations quite so easily. He will have accepted and internalized patterns of behaviour, authoritative propositions and Gospel values. He will act in accordance with this internalized code because he has come to accept these values, not because he needs them to keep control.

By contrast, the first type of person will always be unsure of himself. He lacks the knowledge or the authority - at least that is what he thinks. I am convinced that the faithful have no problem with a bishop or a priest who speaks with conviction about God or the Church and presents his arguments with respect. People immediately sense that he speaks with integrity and from personal experience. They may not agree with him, but such disagreement will not usually generate personal friction, let alone hostility or conflicts.

I once had to dismiss an employee. It was not for personal reasons - in fact I rather liked him. A year later I met him. I was happy to see him and approached to shake his hand. He turned away and said: 'we are no longer friends.' 'Perhaps that is so', I said, 'but is that a reason for us to be enemies?' He relented and agreed. We shook hands. If things go wrong it is usually because priests approach people with the wrong attitude, treat them with disrespect or have not learned to communicate. If the priest has unworthy secondary motivations, people will quickly sense it! They are instinctively put off, even if they cannot articulate the reasons for their feeling. They somehow know that this man does not practice what he preaches.

When conflicts arise and become public knowledge we can safely say that usually they have something to do with tensions in the pastor's personality. But there is more to it. Inconsistencies can also play an important, perhaps even painful, part in one's personal as well as one's public life (see previous chapter). On the other hand parishioners sometimes approach their priests in an unfair or improper manner by expecting from him what he, as a representative of the Church, simply cannot give no matter how much he is pressured. Parish councils or individual councillors may also want to rule the roost, and can easily give the impression that they expect the clergy simply to do as they are told.

A balanced and well trained priest will be able to handle such things in a Christian way, even if it puts a strain on him. It is important for the priest as well as the future parish where he will work, that each candidate is well prepared to handle such situations, ready and able to serve his people yet remain reasonably at ease with it all. This presupposes an adequate degree of personal formation and self-awareness, however. Mostly these two things are found together: successful work and personal happiness. As a Dutch Minister of Agriculture once said: 'be good to the animals and they will be good to you'.

Careful preparation for ministry requires training to be rigorous and demanding, especially in the field of psycho-spiritual integration, so that candidates can be properly prepared for their role as future leaders in the Church. Any institute which sets high standards for ordination must first set itself high standards in teaching and the support offered to candidates as they go through a challenging process of growth towards maturity.

It is obviously not possible to address all the factors that can influence a candidate's formation in a six year period. I will therefore limit myself to those aspects which strike me as most significant in the priestly formation of mature men. There will be an unavoidable overlap and repetition of examples used in earlier chapters. And some of what I am talking about may be equally relevant to working with younger students.

The Teaching Staff

The Bovendonk Institute has a faculty of five members: two full-time staff, the Rector and the Dean of Studies, and three part-time, the Spiritual Director and two coordinators. The coordinators are pastoral theologians who take care of the practical pastoral placements, one for priests, one for deacons. This distribution of oversight has proved to be quite effective, particularly in terms of initial assessment: each faculty member has a chance to interview the candidate from their own perspective and area of expertise. The Spiritual Director assesses the candidate's spiritual journey, the placement co-ordinator looks at his participation in parish life and the dean of studies can assess previous studies and intellectual ability.

At Bovendonk, the Rector retains overall responsibility for decisions on each candidate, but in addition has the task of making an assessment of the psychological maturity of the person. Observations from these initial interviews are then discussed at a faculty meeting at which the critical questions asked are (1) whether this particular person is a suitable candidate for the priesthood and (2) whether our type of training is the best suited for this particular person or would he do better instead at one of the other training institutes'.

Choosing the Staff

Because the average age of most of our candidates is about forty, I have always believed that at least some of the staff and the lecturers should also be older people. Age, of course, is no guarantee of maturity, solid faith or wisdom; but nevertheless, older students should be able to see at least some of the staff as fellow-travellers on the same spiritual journey. As time goes on, however, it has proved increasingly difficult to find such senior staff. This is because there is a whole generation appears to be missing among the clergy: today's new priests are the successors to their grandfathers, and the grandfathers are now aging and disappearing.

When Bovendonk first started, and for quite a number of years thereafter, there was a fair-sized group of energetic senior clergy and lecturers who could be invited to help. Many qualified priests and laity shared the aspirations of the founders and gave enthusiastic support. But as they disappeared from the scene their place has necessarily been taken by younger academics. These people are highly competent and we could not manage without them. Yet it is not only knowledge that must be passed on; wisdom is just as important and age can have wisdom of its own. Further, the training of priests and deacons cannot be left entirely to lay-people. It takes priests to train priests and deacons to train deacons. But this is precisely where we meet a serious practical problem, in that our training takes place over weekends when ordained ministers are most busy in the parish.

Women on the Staff

There have to be women among the lecturers, the counsellors and the supervisors. This is not because we want to promote the role of women in the Church for its own sake, but because women have a different perspective. It has happened several times that other male members of staff have agreed to advise a student to withdraw from the course, but then a woman counsellor has intervened to head this off. Often, it has later become clear that this was precisely the right decision.

A woman counsellor can ask questions or challenge candidates on matters that men would never countenance. A Rector, for example, would rarely challenge a student about their appearance; the women staff do! Many women have a religious sensitivity which can sometimes surprise the male of the species. Women counsellors and supervisors will also often sense immediately how a candidate will relate to women parishioners after. Further, some students find it easier to speak openly to women rather than men. So, we must have women on the staff. I have noticed that the presence of wives at different events on the deacon's programme also has a similar positive effect, especially on the candidates for priesthood - hard to define, but very healthy, even if it happens only once in a while.

Transference and counter transference

Something must also be said about the inner needs of the faculty, especially those who have frequent in-depth contact with students. Unlike training institutes for younger candidates, there is little difference in age at Bovendonk between lecturers and students. So, it is not uncommon for visitors to mistake the staff for students or *vice versa*. We are used to it and it can often lead to certain hilarity.

But on the other hand this similarity in age can also mean friendships can be established which may interfere with the responsibility of staff to supervise and assess candidates. I therefore insist on a certain formality in terms of staff-student relationship – for example, I am called 'Rector' and will always use formal titles and forms of address. It can sometimes feel like a game, but people usually recognise that it is important to maintain working relationships.

Most candidates know this from their professional experience. They also know that a working relationship does not necessarily mean personal distance. Staff members and lecturers must relate openly and objectively with students, if only to guarantee each person the freedom they need to work through the inevitable tensions that are bound to arise. If a staff member becomes a friend, this is bound to interfere with productive working relationships, in that students are less likely to be as open and honest as they must be for fear of losing a friend. By doing this the student misses out on the opportunity to work through those aspects of his personality that require some attention. In short, if staff member seeks friendship with a student, he may be taking away part of the student's freedom.

This is important for all the faculty members, but especially for the Rector: the faculty represents 'authority' and must maintain its responsibility in a professional manner. It often happens that unconscious transference of feelings and perceptions from candidates to the Rector have had a negative impact on relationships. This is to be expected, but the advantage of professional detachment is that students still have the space they need to work through these feelings with a counsellor or supervisor. Some students may try to hide their feelings, negative or positive, towards the Rector; but the mature ones will be ready to acknowledge and explore such feelings directly with the person concerned and this, of course, is always the healthier option.

This way of maintaining professional relationships during training also helps to head off potential problems after ordination when the chairman of the parish council or the bishop become similar targets for transference. By this time, the student should have learned to handle situations like this with some competence, without running the transference script in either a positive or negative way.[64]

It can also happen the other way round - that a staff member does not recognize or understand his own psychological dynamics sufficiently. This can result in unrecognized counter-transference by, for example, taking personal offence at the anger of the student and making sure the student knows it. By assuming the role of a father with a naughty boy, the staff member can then effectively block off the way for the student to deal with the authority issue in a more mature fashion. Instead of solving the problem, the faculty member has now confirmed and reinforced the student's worst fears. Exactly the same can happen with more positive feelings. Both are something that counsellors and supervisors need to watch carefully.

---

[64] There is an excellent study in Dutch on this subject in Boswijk-Hummel, R., *Liefde in Wonderland: Overdracht en tegenoverdracht in de hulprelatie*, Haarlem, DeToorts, 1997.

The staff are there for the students, the students are not there for the faculty

Some would say that such issues should not arise in mature students. This is far from the case. The amount of interaction with part-time students may be less, but the questions are exactly the same as those presented by full-time seminarians. Problems of this kind are just as statistically predictable as anything else. It is simply matter of charity, therefore, to give everyone the room needed to name their inner demons and learn to cope with them.

A faculty member does not go on holiday with 'his' students, he does not have to respond to the attempts some students will make to become overly-familiar, nor does the staff member have to discuss his own personal problems with students and so collude in psychological dependency. There is something wrong when faculty members have unrecognised psychological drivers, such as the need for recognition, appreciation or intimacy, the desire to foster dependency in students, and so on - still less the more manipulative drivers such as counter transference, revenge or control. Such unrecognized needs will soon drive faculty members into unhealthy relationships which in turn will ensure that the system is geared up to feed staff needs rather than the healthy spiritual and pastoral formation of the student.

In a somewhat painful interview, a student once accused me of lacking in pastoral sensitivity. My response was that my function as far as he was concerned was to serve as Rector and not a pastor, and that the purpose of the exercise was to enable him to become a better pastor. The primary responsibility of the Rector is there to promote the spiritual, personal, and theological growth the students need for ministry. The Rector is not there to provide friendship or to form a mutual appreciation society.

No wonder it is so difficult to find clergy or others who are prepared to help with the training of future priests. It is not always easy to deal with the hostile or angry feelings which sometimes come to the surface when one has to make difficult judgements about the future of those who have clear views about their call to ministry and who have already made enormous sacrifices to serve the Church.

There is a price to pay

I must admit I have not always found it easy to follow my own advice and resist the temptation to befriend students who are more or less my own age. Not only does this affect relationships during training, it can also have a knock-on effect and make it particularly difficult to re-establish a friendship of equals after ordination. It is not always easy to change gear suddenly when the student becomes a colleague. Nor is the transition that easy for students, who have experienced me as an authority figure for six years during training.

My own attitude has been shaped by considerable experience as a psychological counsellor working with priests and religious from across our small country. I know only too well the dangers of unprofessional collusion. It always takes a special effort to make new friends outside one's normal circle of acquaintances. But it is especially difficult to change relationships and become friends with those for whom we once had a degree of official oversight. What I want to say is that it can be lonely at the top. Responsibility for the spiritual growth and development of others carries a cost. The question then, is, can I take it? Am I prepared to do all this? And, for how long can I sustain it?

Good will is not enough

Good intentions are not enough when taking on responsibility for training of future priests. It requires a particular set of personal qualities as well as practical skills, and thus demands careful training for all those involved. Only people who know their own limits and inner needs, and who have learned to deal with them, can be allowed to take on this role in a seminary like ours. This does not mean that everything has to be perfect. All human activity is fallible and must remain utterly dependent on the grace of God. But the students themselves, and the people of God over whom they will have pastoral charge, are entitled to know that their clergy have been properly trained by qualified people. No one should be asked to take on this responsibility unless they are properly equipped.

Speaking for myself, even though I had the privilege of a good training (thank God!), I still found it far from easy to stand in front of a group of students, many older than myself and some with much higher qualifications. This was even more difficult when I first started at Bovendonk, because many of the senior students did not like the changes I felt it was important to introduce, and they were not afraid to say so. Younger students tend to look up to a person. But mature students are used to holding their ground. During my first two years at the Institute, I often felt unsure and I suspect I probably would not have coped without the support of several experienced senior staff.

I treasure the memory of the support they gave me and remember them often in my prayers. Equally important was the unconditional support of my bishop. It makes an enormous difference to know there is someone behind you who supports you and with whom you can speak freely. It is also important to recognize the need to accept your own mistakes and learn from them. I certainly made some and sometimes came to realize it later. For a job like this, it is important to work in a team with people who share more or less the same philosophy. Given all this daunting and soul-searching responsibility, it is perhaps not surprising that so few priests are prepared to launch into this adventure of priestly formation.

Nevertheless, my experience as Rector and faculty member at Bovendonk has convinced me that this is one of the most rewarding and enriching vocations in the Church. It is profoundly moving to communicate with people at a deep level about matters of critical importance to their own self-understanding. You recognise in them things you see in yourself – some feelings you did not even realize were there. It is often a mutual process of growth in self-awareness. You see God at work in someone else in ways you had not considered possible, and that can only deepen your own spiritual understanding.

Confronting grown men takes courage

Sometimes you meet a candidate who is not used to someone else saying 'no'. Such people are used to having things their own way whether by charm, gentle manipulation or apparent flexibility. This kind of person often expects preferential treatment, in the diocese and in the parish, and will probably expect it to stay that way. Even experienced members of staff can be taken in by such people and walk straight into the trap. Such a person rarely likes to have this pattern of behaviour pointed out and suddenly feels vulnerable and exposed. Still it must be done, and sooner or later the staff have to take the plunge and confront the person with his behaviour. Individual members of staff must not be deterred by the prospect of being unpopular. With young students this is much easier, but with people of one's own age or older it can be daunting. A lot then depends on the way the staff member is able to cope with their own need for popularity.

Peer Group Support

Mature students naturally challenge each other about their behaviour, attitudes or general outlook. There is nothing wrong with this peer-group interaction and a little more might even be healthy. Unfortunately, students on a part-time programme are only together for two days every two weeks. If there is something in the other person that irritates another student, it is only for a short time; so, he lets it go. In a residential situation things are different. If things get out of hand, feelings quickly run high.

I do not like to think what could have happened if our students had spent longer periods in residence. I have thought about trying it but it proved impossible to organise. Still, there is enough opportunity built into the programme for personal and group interaction to allow personality conflicts to come to the surface. This became particularly evident, I thought, when diaconal candidates joined the course. These new students were generally a bit older, married, and often parents or even grandparents.

In due course, however, the quality and level of conversation between students rose noticeably and feedback became more frequent. By feedback, I mean that the new students found it easier to point out the positive qualities in other students, touching on qualities the individuals concerned may not have even recognised. The dynamics of the group became more mature, more adult. The presence of older married men had a positive influence on the younger students as well: those who had been a little dependent or deferential towards the staff gradually developed a more independent attitude.

This is an entirely good thing. Perhaps they did not always notice it, perhaps it would even surprise them to read this, but the change was unmistakable. Married students have the stability of a relationship and often parental responsibilities. They have a stronger home-life on which to fall back. Although their decision to serve the Church as ordained ministers adds a new dimension to their experience, nevertheless, much of their existing life remains intact.

Students for the priesthood face a far greater challenge as they commit themselves exclusively to the Church. When they join the seminary and are ordained their entire life will change. This higher personal investment can leave candidates more anxious to please the authorities who decide on ordination. They have far more at stake than the diaconal candidates. Indeed, younger students in full-time seminaries can appear deferential if not submissive at times. It is important to remember the psychological context in which such students find themselves.

If these submissive habits are internalized they may well lead to problems in later life, unless they are recognized and dealt with. The diocese of Essen, Germany, once had a vocation campaign with the slogan: 'Wir brauchen keine frommen Jungs. Wir brauchen Priester' which means, 'We do not need pious boys, we need priests' I must say that our students are pretty good in this respect and they keep each other on the right track!

Admissions

The first task for the faculty is management of the admissions' process. This involves two things: a general assessment of the suitability of the man for ordination and then the issue of the most appropriate form of training for this particular candidate. But there are other players in the field as well. Those responsible for formation in the diocese or religious order are just as involved as the staff at Bovendonk. They must also be persuaded that there is a reasonable chance for this person to move through training towards eventual ordination. And that is easier said than done.

Bovendonk only accepts students who are sponsored by a diocese or religious order. As a result, the candidate has to pass through two separate selection processes. Even if a diocese or order recognizes the potential in a candidate, Bovendonk still retains the freedom to accept or refuse that person. Our central concern will be his suitability for our particular approach to formation. So, in addition to the interviews and psychological assessments carried out in the diocese, the candidate has to be interviewed again in Bovendonk where he will also be required to attend a number of week-ends.

Each diocese and order has its own distinctive process for selection. The danger is that this can become too subjective and arbitrary. I would personally be in favour of developing a selection process similar to that used in the Church of England, at least as a backup system to provide addition support for bishops. In the Church of England, candidates go through an initial screening process with *Diocesan Directors of Ordination* (DDO) and if it is thought appropriate they are then referred to a national Selection Conference or Bishops' Advisory Panel. This conference lasts for the inside of a week. During that time, a team of selectors from different dioceses and disciplines interview each candidate. The results of the different tests, interviews and experience of simply living together in the group are sent to the relevant diocesan bishop together with the advice of the team.

But in the absence of such a national system, the faculty at Bovendonk share the screening process. One faculty member talk to candidates about their parish involvement. Another then explores the person's spiritual life, whilst a third will look at his academic background - his intellectual achievements and ambitions.

As Rector, I then focus primarily on matters of personality and maturity and the way these affect faith, work, relations with others and the Church. I will also draw on the observations and feedback from other faculty members where appropriate. These first impressions remain relevant not just for the admissions process, but also as a foundation for further work thereafter.

Responsibility for one's own vocation

God calls whom He wills. God calls when and where and in the way He wills. It is not up to seminary staff to second guess a genuine vocation. Within the framework laid down by the *Magisterium* of the Church, we listen to the candidate's story, try to assess his motivation, and in the light of that evaluation try to form a judgement about the potential offered by that person to respond to the call he feels he has experienced. But in the end, it remains the responsibility of the bishop to confirm and validate that vocation by accepting a candidate for ordination.

The candidate is not the object, but the subject of his training. Formation has to equip him with the resources he will need to grow into an effective priest or deacon, but it is his responsibility to make good use of these resources. There was a time, not so long ago, when those responsible for formation in dioceses and in religious orders tended to make training as easy as possible for candidates, to lower the bar in order to be as flexible and attractive as possible for fear of putting them off.

All this was the mirror image of the traditional approach, where the superior insisted that candidates knock three times on the door to test if they really were seeking God. I am not advocating a return to these older practices, but we must keep things in perspective. It is the candidate who says he is called by God. It is the candidate who says he wants to serve God through his Church as a priest or deacon. So also it is up to the candidate to show that he can meet the criteria laid down by the Church for ordination. Sometimes you have to explain carefully to the candidate why admission to a seminary is simply not the same as admission to a university or a professional training programme.

The consequences of incardination

Joining a seminary is not the same as enrolling at a university or theological faculty even if some students find themselves with a foot in both camps (for example, if candidates live in a hostel [*convitto*] but study at university). In contrast to lay ministers, priests and deacons are incardinated in a diocese. This creates not only a spiritual bond with the bishop, but also an obligation on the bishop to provide his priests and deacons with a living.

Initially, this means the diocese (that is, the faithful) will have to carry most of the cost of the six-year programme of formation. Thereafter, if the candidate continues, there will be the life-long bond between the diocese and the minister. The bishop is responsible for providing good clergy for the people. But on top of that, he must also ensure that the candidate is willing and able to live out the obligations he has taken on through ordination.

At ordination, the candidate commits himself to 'assist the bishop loyally in the pastoral care of God's People, to preside at the liturgy in accordance with the traditions of the Church, to preach the Word of God, to explain the Catholic Faith diligently, and to bind himself to Christ the High Priest'. The candidate moreover places his hands in those of the bishop and he promises 'respect and obedience to the bishop and his successors'.[65] Even before this, the future priest has already committed himself to live a celibate life. Not a trifling matter, to be sure, and all this has to be carefully explained *before* the student is admitted onto the course, unless it already has been clearly spelled out at some early point in the process such as a vocational retreat.

Nothing can be taken for granted

These days, it cannot be assumed that younger candidates, or even older ones, know much about the Catholic faith, let alone the ordained ministry. It is not uncommon for some men to present themselves as potential students without having the slightest idea what is involved. It is not enough to ask questions; these people must also be given simple basic information about the Church, the ministry and the formation process. Even the most elementary things need to be explained.

In the past, men who applied for the seminary had an active Catholic background, were familiar with the liturgy and Catholic practices, had some idea about the Church, and knew their catechism. This is no longer the case. If we only admitted students who already are familiar with Catholic teaching, liturgical customs and structures, then the number of first year students will dwindle even further.

Taking the home seriously

In some cases, aspirants are anxious to start straightaway. It can annoy or disappoint them to be asked if they have really thought through the practical consequences of joining the seminary. It then becomes clear in some cases that, in spite of their protestations, they have not really thought through all the issues. On occasion, I have had to advise married men who applied for training as deacons not to do so while they have pre-school age children or young teenagers. Experience generally suggests that

---

[65] See the Roman Pontifical, '*The ordination of deacons, priests and bishops*'.

children in these age groups especially need a father, and just as important, wives need their husbands to help with the care of the children. The same may also hold for other school-age children as well.

All married candidates need to realize that being away from home for 21 weekends a year will almost certainly have more of an impact on their family than they realise. Similarly, serious consideration must be given to the wife's attitude: does she support her husband in his call to become a deacon? A home visit is thus an essential part of the admissions' process. On more than one occasion, a man who appeared eminently suited for the diaconate had to withdraw because it later became clear that the wife had changed her mind about the changes ahead, despite her initial consent. She begins to sense that all his talk of ministry has been one-sided – his "show and not hers", as one person put it.

Mixed marriages of deacons

There are a surprising number of candidates for the diaconate who are married to Protestants. Many of these partners wish to remain active in their own Church communities, and this can lead to unforeseen complications. Catholic regulations stipulate that a married man can only be ordained deacon if his wife signs a declaration of consent; yet, as a Protestant, the wife cannot take an active role in her husband's faith community.

Sooner or later, the husband is bound to go and lead worship in 'his' Catholic Church while the wife goes off to 'her' Church. Normally, these spouses usually work out some form of compromise, but the practical implications still need to be given serious thought throughout formation. This would actually be an interesting question for further research: to what extent does the active involvement of the wife in a Protestant community have an impact on the husband's understanding of the role of the deacon in the Roman Catholic Church?

Recent bereavements

Something else I have begun to recognize is how many men come forward for ordination within a year or two of bereavement – for example, men who have felt a sense of vocation for some time, but have put it off because a sense of responsibility towards a sick mother. This is surely a laudable reason for delaying, and there are probably many other similar situations. Another fairly common pattern is that someone who has had no contact with the Church, or who has drifted away over the years, suddenly presents himself after the intense experience of bereavement for ordination either as a priest or deacon.

Such an applicant will often see no connection between loss and the 'emergence of vocation', still less recognise the feelings of guilt often generated by the death of a close relative. Did I do all I could to help the person who died, relieve their suffering, show my affection? Were we able to work through any unfinished business before the death? Was my behaviour in anyway reprehensible? Similar thoughts may linger just below the surface of consciousness, but they make the person feel that they need to make reparation in some way, perhaps by doing something 'noble' such as serving God in His Church.

The impact of recent bereavement on those exploring a new vocation thus needs to be considered carefully. The (unconscious) real Latent Self still has too much of a hold on the (proclaimed) ideal Personal Self. I am not saying this is always the case, but it happens often enough to highlight the need for caution in conducting interviews. Initial conversations will soon make it clear whether or not the person in question is wrestling with post-bereavement guilt and if so, the candidate obviously needs to be made aware of what is going on. I can think of at least four men who came to recognize the effect these guilt-feelings were having on their sense of call to ministry during the course of an admission interview. Having recognised the situation, they wisely decided to put off any further consideration until they had adequately dealt with these hidden psychological pressures.

A realistic view of the Church is required

Although numbers are now steadily declining, there are still older candidates who can remember 'the good old days' when things were different in both Church and society. In my early years as Rector of Bovendonk the older students were constantly talking about the 1960's. By coincidence, two of them discovered that in 1968 one had stood on the barricades while the other had been on duty as a police officer trying to control the riot. Now here they both were on the same side, wanting to become priests. Similarly, a few students in my early years were members of Opus Dei, while others had supported the Eighth of May movement.[66] The rest of the students were spread right across the spectrum of different views and perspectives. In due course, however, the extremes gradually began to come together, especially as new students added to the mix each year.

Today, it must be said, there still are differences among the students, but they are less marked than ten years ago. As students from Gröningen to Antwerp come to Bovendonk we get a fair representation of life in the Church in the Low Countries. A few students are between 50 and 60 years old, others between 30 and 40. Often, the older ones come from more traditional backgrounds. They sometimes have a hard time, because the younger generation, without intending to be judgemental, have little experience or understanding of older ways.

The average student wants to be an 'ordinary' Catholic (as they would put it), and it irritates him to hear an older lecturer talking about the 'good old days'. It is important when interviewing new candidates, therefore, to examine their image of the Church. Several times a student dropped out in the first year simply because he discovered that his image of the Church and ordained ministry simply did not match the reality for which Bovendonk was preparing him.

Ironically some students in their thirties now have an equally illusory image of the pre-conciliar Church, something they have never, of course, experienced themselves. Such candidates usually opt for an alternative programme. In any case, we try our best to challenge the illusion or turn them down if they persist.

This is what we called in a previous chapter the problem of dissonance between the 'Ideal Institutional Self' and the 'Ideal Personal Self'. In other words, we look for the degree of consistency between the ideal to which the candidate aspires and the expectations he thinks the Church will place on him as a priest or deacon. If it looks unlikely that the dissonance will be resolved in a realistic period of time, then you have a real

---

[66] A protest movement in the Dutch Catholic Church following the visit of Pope John Paul II, in 1985, when speakers selected by lay movements were not allowed to deliver their speeches in the Pope's presence.

problem. Such a student is almost certainly presenting a form of rigid romanticism.

Pastoral effectiveness and perfectionism

The students who come to Bovendonk often have professional backgrounds and that means they have held responsible positions and are trained to solve problems. They may have a commercial background, or they may have worked in the caring professions (health care, elder care, education, and so forth). They are trained to get the best possible result at the lowest possible cost in the shortest possible time. Time is money. Priestly formation has to break this habit, but a key question is whether the student is able to make the necessary change. God's grace often works through the ministry of a priest. This gift of grace may not depend on the individual, but the minister nevertheless has to do his bit (see Chapter One).

This requires a degree of 'passivity', that is to say, an ability to let go of one's need to keep things under control and to learn to trust in God more than in personal skills. This means learning to 'waste' hours in prayer and meditation. It means simply being with people who suffer or grieve without trying 'to do' anything. It means learning to accept that inaction is sometimes a virtue. A minister of God's grace is not omnipotent and cannot solve all problems. He often must be content with simply being there. In short, the future priest has to go through a conversion process from 'solving' problems to *attending* to problems; a conversion process from 'a man who realizes things in first place to a man who is carrier of the Mystery in first place.

This conversion process takes time, but right from the start, an assessment must be made about the candidate's ability to negotiate transition. This is where it becomes critically important to listen for the 'perfectionist streak' in what the candidate says about himself. It is remarkable how many people in the Church are 'perfectionists', although they will readily admit human fallibility. Perfection simply is not possible in this world. They find it easy to say this about other people but not so easy to apply it to themselves. Of course, we all try to do the best we can, and we may hope that others will do the same, recognising all the time that reality is likely to be very different.

Perfectionism is usually a coping mechanism. People are not really trying to reach an impossible ideal; rather, they are trying desperately to avoid mistakes. Mistakes trigger in them the fear of losing esteem and therefore affection. Perhaps failure will mean they become the target of criticism. Rejection is what they really fear: a loss of respect from those in authority whose affirmation they crave.

Guilt feelings, often linked to denial or repression of aggression, are painful and must therefore be avoided at all costs. How can this be done? One way is through activism, trying to achieve the impossible - in other words, perfectionism. Paradoxically, if they really want to be good priests, they must learn to live with imperfection, which is really only another word for humility. Will the student come to accept imperfection in himself and others as a reasonable norm in life?[67]

The candidate may also have other positive qualities he has acquired through his profession but sometimes even these can stand in the way of effective pastoral ministry. Teachers, for example, are used to talking and explaining everything. Once a priest, the former teacher must learn to listen more and speak less. Or men trained in the physical sciences or in technology may not have developed the sensitivity or empathy required for the exercise of pastoral care.

---

[67] Mt. 5,48 says: 'You, therefore, must be perfect, as your heavenly Father is perfect'. The word *teleios* is usually translated as 'perfect'. *Teleios* means 'aimed at a purpose', 'knowing the limits', 'blameless', 'mature, adult, full-grown, ready', or 'reaching completion through purification'. 'Perfection' is too easily taken to mean something free of imperfection. Many feelings, automatic reactions and emotions are felt to be disturbing, threatening, socially unacceptable, or signs of weakness, and consequently they are often repressed or denied. To be full-grown or mature means, in fact, to be a real human being complete with all the 'weaknesses' that are part of the human condition. Hence the paradoxical conclusion: in order to be 'full-grown' some people must learn to be 'imperfect'. Perhaps we can interpret Jesus admoniton to mean: purify your objectives, do not pursue all sorts of things and aim at being fully grown.

Surrender or self-determination

There is another related point concerning older candidates that also needs attention. Having been in positions of responsibility, many mature students have learned to stand on their own two feet. As with other professional skills acquired through experience, this quality can be a great advantage; priests are expected to show leadership and exercise authority. The modern world, however, also puts too high a value on personal autonomy. Right from infancy, young people are strongly encouraged to develop a sense of self-determination and sometimes this can be overdone. It teaches some people to be unduly defensive about their 'personal space' and generates a certain inflexibility in terms of the world around them. They may talk easily about generalities and impersonal matters, but the moment you try to get onto more serious matters of self-awareness, they close down.

It is obvious that no one is going to open up straightaway in a new relationship and disclose the most intimate secrets of their being. If they did, most other people would consider them unbalanced if not disturbed. But at the other extreme, the candidate who is still unable to open out after several interviews and resists every attempt to explore deeper personal issues presents a problem. If everything is 'private', how can such a person ever expect to develop the trust needed to sustain a life-long relationship of trust between a priest and, for example, his bishop?

This resistance to self-disclosure also raises interesting questions about future pastoral relationships. Will such a priest ever be able to build up trusting relationships with parishioners, or for that matter, with God? It is evident that between these two extremes lies an endless spectrum of possibility between privacy and openness. It is about trust: if someone generally feels safe, he will usually start to open up, especially if he comes to believe that the interviewer is not just being inquisitive but really wants to help them come to a deeper self-knowledge and a more affective relationship with other people and with God. Some people want to be more open, but just find it difficult to step over the threshold.

Others have no desire to change at all. They have simply decided that they want to become priests and expect the ordination to take place tomorrow. They have nothing to learn but how to swing the thurible. They will speak (nobly!) about 'letting oneself be ordained', without any real sense that others might want to have a say in the process. This need for self-determination can have dramatic consequence: more than once, students who have gradually discovered what the priesthood really means then back off as they sense the threat to their personal autonomy. Remember the young man of Luke 18!

This can even happen to people the staff feel have the potential to become good priests. Such inner conflict, whether serious or apparently superficial, demand careful and patient attention to help the candidate come to a responsible decision. Training a person is not always a success story. I remember one case in particular. In spite of his good intentions, one candidate withdrew from training, disappointed like his counterpart in the Gospel. He was sad because he knew he wanted to be a priest and that he should be a priest. His problem was, however, that he could not let go of his certainties. You may be tempted to ask: does the Lord not give all the grace needed to follow his call? The truth is that God always seems to respect human freedom, and the story of the love relationship between God and humanity is and must remain an unfathomable mystery.

Affective-sexual dimension

When the subject of celibacy and sexuality is raised in the pre-admission interview, the interviewer normally encounters some degree of reluctance, if not defensiveness, on the part of the candidate. To be honest, the interviewer is unlikely to relish this moment either - if he does, he probably needs to see a counsellor as well! In many of these interviews, however, it is clear that the candidate has found a certain inner peace. He has reached a point of integration in that area of his life. Indeed, older candidates often have had experiences and sometimes a rather active sex-life, and they may be entirely at ease talking about such things.

The unpleasant reality is that you have to delve deeply into such matters, if only to avoid of the danger of admitting someone who is likely at some point in the future to commit sexual abuse. But in any case, at a more immediate level, the Church authorities are entitled to have a sense of each candidate's commitment to celibacy. Concerns around sexuality become even more important if a prospective candidate seems abnormally reluctant to talk about the subject. This reluctance could easily be masking all sorts of inner conflicts.

The important issue here is not so much any specific episode of sexual misbehaviour as the underlying psychological motivation – for example, power, dependency or aggression. If we ask about these things, we may well be told that this is no business of the Church. But if we do not ask about them and the priest turns out to be a petty dictator or involved in the sexual abuse of children or manipulates pastoral relationships in other ways, then the training institution has not done its work and the Church is held accountable. Sadly, widespread publicity about recent scandals provides a plethora of examples

It is important to note, however, that many of the unsavoury activities which have understandably caught the headlines in recent years have usually been building up for years – often as long as 50 or 60 years. That does not make them less traumatic for the victims, but it is important to keep all such dramatic events in perspective. The majority of the clergy never have been, and probably never will be, involved in them. What continues to intrigue me is the fact that justified indignation appears to be directed more towards the attempt by the Church to sweep things under the carpet rather than outrage caused by the actual incident.

Nevertheless, publicity has blown the lid off the cesspool, and that can only be good. It has also forced training institutions and Church authorities to face the issue properly, although it must be admitted that this is not yet universally true. During a workshop on sexual abuse in Rome, Msgr. Stephan J. Rossetti, at that time President of St. Luke Institute in Silver Spring, Maryland, presented a list of questions he suggested needed to be considered in relation to every candidate. He argued that careful attention to the fine detail of answers given is the only way to get an adequate insight into a person's affective-sexual development. Without this careful attention to detail, there was little hope of discovering any latent problems; and yet I suspect that if we attempted to use this questionnaire in the Netherlands, we would quickly run into an official roadblock because of the laws on privacy!

This is an issue which still needs to be resolved. Perhaps it will never be resolved in the Netherlands because of the different admission systems working across the dioceses. A few very intrusive questions would have to be put to every single candidate in each diocese in exactly the same way. As mentioned above, all candidates in the Church of England have to go through the same process, including psychological tests, as part of a standard procedure. I cannot see this happening in the Church in the Netherlands. It would likewise be pointless trying to hire psychological consultants to do the testing for us for they would be bound by professional confidentiality and could never tell us anything useful.

Ideally, candidates who are walking around with seriously dark corners in their lives would come to the obvious conclusion that they are ready to become priests even unless they are willing to seek help. In practice, things are different; no matter how hard you try, no system is foolproof. In any case, It is a fact that some 'dark shadows', or latent affective forces will only come to the surface after ordination. To be sure, the odds on this happening in ordinands with an average age of 43 are considerably smaller than men with an average age of 24, but you can never be certain. I repeat, age is no guarantee of maturity, and occasionally someone of 24 is more mature than a 70 year old. How any new priest deals with unfolding affective forces depends on his personal profile – the degree of honesty and openness, his strength of character, his faith, his conscience and the extent to which he has internalized successfully the values central to his vocation, and so on. But these psychological dimensions can be assessed during initial training and they provide a good indicator of the candidate's affective disposition.

Finally, there is the unavoidable question of the candidate's sexual orientation. This one is comparatively easy to deal with in the Dutch context. Candidates for Bovendonk have reached the age where they tend to know themselves quite well. When I first became Rector in 1995, twelve years ago now, I had come from Brazil and Rome where, at that time, men did not easily talk about such things. It therefore took me by surprise to hear aspirants in the Netherlands could speak about their homo- or hetero-sexual orientation in a simple, direct and relaxed way. It took some getting used to!

I soon discovered in conversations with bishops that the only thing that really concerned them was the issue of celibacy: was the candidate in fact already established in a celibate lifestyle? This is all the Church asks, and this is the commitment they will take on at their ordination. So this is what we have told the students. Each person has their own conscience and each person has to make their own decision.

No one can decide how someone else should live, and most people would not want to know, let alone try control the sexuality of another. Once we have made our choice, we must live with it in a responsible and consistent way. That applies just as much to older candidates as to younger men. The priest is called to build bridges between people, and between people and God. He must be able to relate to others, male and female, in an unselfish and respectful way. If he remains ambivalent about his own sexuality, if his self image is any way unrealistic or uncertain, if his private life is not consistent with his priestly vocation, then he will be seen to be lacking in authenticity. He will constantly have to live with tensions that will not only disturb his personal spiritual life, but also undermine his priestly and pastoral activity.

Team work

The ability to work effectively in teams is of the utmost importance in the contemporary social context. Pastoral work is intrinsically collaborative, as clergy are called to work with laymen and women, paid staff and volunteers, as well as ordained colleagues. All clergy will, therefore, unavoidably find themselves as members of teams, leading teams, or learning to manage and organize teams. Some people, of course, simply do not have the skills needed for this work. In this case, the best thing they can do is let someone else who has the required skills take on the leadership role.

The model of the autocratic parish priest of olden days is no longer viable and candidates for the priesthood need to know this right from the start. It still happens that some hang on to that romantic image somewhere at the back of their minds and, consciously or unconsciously, expect sooner or later to move into that position. But it is a fact of life that more and more parishes these days have been formed into clusters and these networks demand a far greater degree of flexibility on the part of clergy.

Priests, deacons, lay-pastoral workers and volunteers have to work closely together, keeping their distinctive roles, to be sure, but seeing their respective responsibilities as part of a wider corporate enterprise. This collegial model of ministry has to be the way to build and maintain healthy communities of faith in order to administer the sacraments and to do whatever else is needed, useful and beneficial.

By virtue of his priesthood, the priest is the leader of a community. But not everyone is a natural leader and if a particular priest lacks the team skills required in contemporary ministry they have a problem. This is often easy to detect in older candidates. All the staff needs to do is ask the candidate about their life experience: what work has he done? What was his role in each of these jobs, and how long did he stay with each employer? Has he done any additional voluntary work and what role has he played in social or other organizations? Spiritual and pastoral leadership has a dynamic of its own and requires its own specific gift. It involves organisation policy development, delivery and follow-up. Not everyone has these skills. Some people are anxious to have the status of leader but lack the capacity to do it!

Rectors of seminaries and other training institutes in the Netherlands meet regularly, and a few years ago the question was raised at one of these meetings: what should trainers be seeking to achieve? Should the goal be the training of priests or the training of vicars? And by vicars, they meant in this context the priests-leaders - managers of the large pastoral units characteristic of the contemporary Church in the Netherlands. By priests, they referred to men who wanted to limit their activities to traditional priestly or sacramental ministry, leaving organizational matters to other people.

Opinion was sharply divided. My own view is that, if possible, priests should try to move into a leadership position in the parish, but I would not want to exclude anybody who has not got the particular skills needed to manage a team. I have to admit that we did turn down one diocesan candidate who refused on principle to have anything to do with parish administration. In today's world, it is essential that priests have some capacity for leadership, or at least be willing to develop some basic skills in that area. The man became a monk instead and is very happy.

It is important to try and understand how well a candidate recognises this in himself. If he does not have this capacity, can he live with the limitations this will impose, and is he able to delegate? Someone who is still rigidly attached to the former romantic ideal of the parish priest and cannot let go, risks paralysing other members of the team who may have a better capacity to organise things. For the good of the community, the priest must learn to let go.

Self-acceptance and self-revelation

Anything that a person has accepted in himself, and that he has integrated into his life, he can also share with other people in an appropriate confidential setting. The less something has been accepted, the more it will be kept repressed; the more a man wants to deny or keep secret, the more he will try to hide. Or, following an expression of Rossetti: 'one is as sick as his secrets'. The paradox indeed is that the more anxiously he tries to hide something, the more he is likely to call attention to the very thing he most wants to avoid. I always say to students: look, if there are things in your past or present life that worry you, talk about it now with the person responsible for your formation, because one day they will have to give advice to the bishop about your suitability for ordination.

Experienced faculty members, those who have had a clinical training, have a knack for noticing if things are not quite right. If the candidate is evasive, or if personal tutors are kept in the dark, it can only generate doubt and perhaps lead to a negative judgement about suitability for ordination. If the man can be open about what is going on in himself, it will at least assure the tutor he is able to talk openly to a suitably qualified person. In such a situation the candidate and his mentor can honestly explore the possibilities – whether he needs more help, or whether his particular situation will have an impact on his future training.

This is not always the case, however. Often it quickly becomes clear that the fear is worse than the problem. And if there are problems, it is better to intervene sooner rather than later, before the candidate goes too far along the road to ordination. If it does become clear that the problem is so evidently incompatible with the life of a priest or deacon, it is better to say so before the candidate has the chance to do any serious damage either to himself or to the community he will serve as an ordained person. And to be fair, such a situation is usually something the candidate himself wants to avoid.

In my twelve years as Rector, I have only once found myself having to make an immediate decision to terminate the training of a candidate, and even then only after consulting his bishop. This is not bad statistic, given the number of candidates who have passed through Bovendonk. There have been a few cases where candidates have been too fearful to open up during the admission process – where the problem has been not so much unacceptable behaviour in a priest but rather anxiety about behaviour that is linked to deeper internal fears related to their personality.

There have been other cases where we could see from the outset that something was not quite right but allowed the candidate to start the course in the hope that the issues would come to the surface in due course. With the benefit of hindsight, we would now have to admit that in one or two cases we should have acted sooner, because it turned out to be far more painful asking someone to withdraw later in course than it would have been to intervene right at the beginning.

The key issue is whether the candidate himself realizes that he has a problem. I try as much as possible to follow the wise counsel delivered in the motto: 'Do not touch a sore spot if you have nothing with which to heal it'. As long as you are not sure about the cause and location of the pain, leave it alone. If somebody later admits that they have held something back, then it is a matter of patiently and carefully exploring the issue and considering the consequences. It is always a good sign if the candidate finds the courage to tell you himself, to open up and take someone else into his confidence.

Dealing with material things

It is not unimportant how people manage money, properties and material things. Older candidates who come forward for priestly formation often have much higher salaries than they will ever get as a priest. Parish councils often complain to the diocese that their newly ordained priest does not know how to handle money

– he takes out loans, lives beyond his means, or buys expensive vestments without prior consultation with the Treasurer.

Some people seem to find it difficult to keep financial records or submit proper proof of expenses incurred. In some cases, it may be a case of wanting to retain a degree of independence. In other cases, it may reflect a desire to maintain a kind of carefree bachelor life. It is a matter of simple common sense to check at an early stage if a candidate has large debts, if only because once he is incardinated his debt reverts to the diocese, that is to say, his 'employer', sometimes leading to serious complications. A candidate may even be addicted to expensive habits. It is therefore important to prepare all the students during training for a future where they will earn considerably less. For this, if for no other reason, part of the admissions process should always be an interview with the Financial Officer of the diocese.

Unfinished previous studies

Another issue requiring attention in the early stages of selection is a candidate's established academic record. This is particularly important if there are gaps or if the person has a habit of starting courses and not finishing them. Several of the students when I became Rector, and several more among the hundred or so I admitted over the following twelve years, had not completed previous courses of study. They did not complete their priestly formation either, not because they were asked to leave but because they once again gave up.

A standard pattern seemed to emerge: a student would do well at college or university and often achieve good grades for their coursework, but would then fail to turn up for the final exams. I did not notice this at first but after the umpteenth example I began to recognize the pattern. I do not want to frighten anyone, let alone exclude people who have gone through this kind of experience, but it does make you wonder.

Why would intelligent men go through a lengthy training only to stop before they finish? I am not aware of any research into this phenomenon and perhaps it has not been done. Nevertheless, I would expect there to be some sort of correlation with at least two of the inner conflicts Erikson identifies: autonomy versus shame/doubt and productivity versus inferiority.[68] The conflict between autonomy and shame/doubt usually occurs when children have been subject to serious inner strain in their second and third year of life. This leads them to be fearful of success and because it might lead to an independence which is perceived as threatening. Success thus has a cost they do not wish to pay. Fear of failure can be another factor - in spite of earlier academic achievement, students like this can be afraid that they cannot do it again. Consequently they back away from the humiliation they fear they may have to face.

A child of primary school age goes through one of the most important phases in personal development as he or she learns how to handle specific tasks, join new groups and develop the habits needed for successful social interaction. Naturally, things can go wrong. Sometimes the child is simply unable to fulfil the expectations of the teaching staff or their peers and starts to experience a sense of inferiority (Erikson's fourth conflict). If so, these feelings are likely to remain until the child discovers other personal resources or learns to cope.

In theory, unfinished academic business from the past should be irrelevant in priestly formation. In practice, however, the deeper psychological motivations that made a candidate abandon earlier studies may still be operative. The old dynamics and feelings of inferiority may still be in place, and the faculty would do well to look carefully at the root of the problem.

A six year formation

Once the decision has been made to admit a candidate, he enters into the regular routine of weekends starting with Vespers at seven on Friday evening and finishing with Midday Prayer and a meal on Sunday. The first year students are not given any other chores so they can get used to the rhythm of the weekends and establish a routine, although they do assist right from the start in the liturgy groups which lead corporate prayer over the weekend with the help of the Spiritual Director. The first year group also organizes a social evening for the traditional Dutch Sinterklaas ('Santa Claus') celebration. This involves, among

---

[68] For the eight stages of development and the conflicts Erikson associated with them see Hall, C.S., & Lindzey, G., *Erik H. Erikson*, in *Theories in Personality*, John Wiley & Sons, New York, 1957 (3rd ed., 1978), pp. 87-100

other things, gentle ragging, and presents an important milestone as they present themselves to, and become full members of the overall student body. After that weekend, no one feels like an outsider anymore!

In mid-November, around the seventh residential weekend, it is usually possible to detect a slight turning in the emotional tide. The novelty has worn off for the first year students as get used to the pattern of busy weekends after a full week's work. The first examinations in January start to appear on the horizon. The year appears to be running along smoothly, but the freshmen are discovering all sorts of things they had barely noticed before. They have to find a personal Spiritual Director from their diocese. They have met each weekend with one of the Bovendonk counsellors to talk about their life, work, family, social life, and the impact of their studies on everything else. The Director of Pastoral Studies makes an appointment to visit the student at home. He shows an interest in the candidates ordinary secular employment and the local parish where they worship.

The married diaconal candidates go through a slightly different process. Their wives and children must get used to their absence every other weekend and to hearing stories about formation. Twice a year, wives will be invited to attend part of the weekend and follow a program of their own. The content of the course, the distinctive ecclesiastical language used, the rhythm of prayer all add to the demands made on the family and can produce a plethora of reaction. When Bovendonk first started training married deacons, there were many complaints about the heavy workload. It was hardly surprising for they had to fit into an existing system which had been designed for single men preparing for the priesthood.

The diocese or religious order of each candidate will also make demands of their own. The student will have to follow an additional program designed to help him grow into the diocese. Candidates who are members of a religious order are said to have it easy. 'They have more time to study.' In reality, however, some of these younger men may have to carry many other responsibilities within in their ageing communities.

Making choices and taking responsibility

Hat off for our students! It is frankly unbelievable what they are able to achieve through their determination and commitment. They rarely miss any of the weekends, even when there are good reasons to do so. And during the Bovendonk residentials they seldom skip lectures or anything else. If someone is missing from prayers or whatever, one of his colleagues will take the initiative to go and find out why. The students know very well what the demands of a part-time programme are and why the weekends are 'sacred'. They are told right at the beginning that they should never ask for permission to miss a weekend, because the answer will always 'no'.

They are told they are old enough and wise enough to judge for themselves if there is an obvious reason why they should miss something. Some individuals will still look for an approving nod, but it never comes. If that means that they feel insecure or guilty, then so be it – it is all part of the process to be worked through. Taking responsibility entails making decisions and students must learn to do this on their own without approval of others.

Occasionally, a student will tell me that he intends to miss several weekends. I then gently remind him that the regulations state that students must attend a minimum of 90% of the course, but point out that I will not make the decision for him. That would simply allow the student to remain 'passive', one of the major dangers in seminary training. Accepting responsibility also means accepting the consequences of one's actions. Those involved in pastoral work know well enough that the demands of parish ministry regularly cut right across family and social commitments and that difficult decisions will have to be made.

Diaconal students in particular can face some hard decisions, especially in the first year. Perhaps they feel they are being asked to give up too much. Perhaps the gap is too great between the way they have understood and lived out their faith in the parish, and all that they are now learning about the realities of the Church and the official structures for ordained ministry. From our point of view, it is of utmost importance that we are crystal clear from the beginning about what it means to be an ordained minister in the Netherlands or Flanders.

Developing an identity and role conflicts

When role conflicts arise, as can happen during the pastoral placement or soon after ordination, it is important to have a strong sense of identity as a deacon or priest (although 'strong' does not mean inflexible or rigid).[69] Ordination confers a specific role in the Church. Team members and parish councils as well as the congregation generally may also attribute to the priest or deacon a role which reflects their understanding of 'Church'. This perceived role does not always fit comfortably with the actual role given by ordination and Church order.

And then there is the profile assumed by the priest or deacon himself, which can vary according individual psychological needs. All these conflicts can be painful: the priest or deacon wants to please everybody, as if the Lord has told him personally to be nice to everyone. This desire to be liked may push the younger cleric to yield to every demand. Sooner or later this will boil over and cause frustration, both for himself and for those around him.

Alternatively, the priest or deacon may retreat into the siege mentality of absolute certainty (by way of counter-reaction) into order to mask his own uncertainty and inability to take criticism and face questioning. In such circumstances, he will be unable to give rational reasons for his point of view but will simply appeal to hierarchy and external authority without any consideration of what other people might think or feel or expect from him. When that happens, the fat really is in the fire and rational communication becomes nearly impossible.

At the other end of the scale is the priest or deacon who buckles under the pressure to conform to the expectations of powerful people in the congregation and then neglects the authority given to him by virtue of his ordination and his place in the Church. The outcome in either case is likely to become a conflict with Church authority. Neither of these situations is healthy. Both can be avoided if priests have a mature sense of their own identity as a person, both as a man and as a pastor.

A mature priest who is questioned about his priesthood or the teachings of the Church will not feel threatened nor feel the need

---

[69] For role conflict in general see, for example, Spiegel, J.P., *The resolution of role conflict within the family*, in M. Greenblatt, D.J. Levinson & R.H. Williams, *The Patient and the Mental Hospital*, New York, Free Press, 1957

to badger others into submission. He will keep the conversation going with everyone and simply make his point clear or proclaim the Good News without thinking he has to force others to accept what he has to say. As previously mentioned, few people today have any problem with clear convictions as long as they are presented in an authentic and balanced way. What counts is the way they are presented.

Where do I stand in the Church?

New students from Flanders (Belgium) sometimes show surprise when they discover that Dutch students feel completely at ease interrupting a lecture to question or debate. This would not be done at home, they say. Some Dutch students and lecturers might feel the same - sometimes a little more of old-fashioned approach might not be such a bad thing, they suggest. A few students keep this up for years. They want the 'right' answer, and will go on asking over and over again, confused by the lecturer who refuses to play the game. But through open discussion and examination all the alternatives they begin to learn how to evaluate the evidence and form convictions of their own. They do learn the official teaching of the Church; but they also learn how to make sense of it. To become truly a person who can speak on behalf of the Church, the student must have considered the key teaching of the *Magisterium*, defined his own position, and internalized them both. If students cannot do this, they will never be able to speak for the Church with a measure of sincerity and authenticity.

If they cannot do this satisfactorily, they must be honest enough to accept the consequences. If you know beforehand you will, for the remainder of your ministry, be expected to defend positions you cannot share, you will be in perpetual conflict. In these cases, perhaps the only honourable way forward is to withdraw so the student can find somewhere else in which he can freely speak his convictions. The dialogue between one's own personal point of view and the official teaching of the Church has to remain a dynamic process of seeking and testing the evidence.

Experience by itself is not enough

Many of the students starting at Bovendonk have not been involved in systematic study for years. They will often, especially in the early stages, appeal to experience. They will argue that book-learning is not really that important. Of course, experience gained from life and from profession expertise is important, but the real issue is what people have *learned* from that experience. Young people learn how to learn; older people learn how to integrate experience into the totality of their life. This is especially true if they go through a massive change such as the transition from secular employment to the life and work of a priest.

At first, there were no examinations in the initial stages of training at Bovendonk, precisely because my predecessors wanted the students to integrate and build on their existing life-experience. But we had to change our ways. Nowadays we have examinations and tests set at the level of higher professional education. There are students on the course who could easily complete a university degree in Theology. They deliberately opted for Bovendonk because they want a practical training orientated towards pastoral ministry in the Church. I think we have achieved this by and large over the 24 years that Bovendonk has been in existence. But we also know there is a need for intellectual formation as well as 'practical know-how'.

Coping with crises

How do we cope with crises? Given that the course lasts six years, it is not surprising that some of the students pass through what might be called a 'crisis'. Nearly every student goes through a period when he feels close to giving up as the inner conflicts and turmoil start to surface, or he feels he does not understand himself any more, or he is simply not at ease. There is nothing wrong with that: in fact, it is only natural and, I would say, necessary.

I would be more worried if a student never went through such a crisis. A man gets new ideas thrown at him, insights that may differ widely from what he has always accepted. It is not surprising if he becomes unsure of himself at times. The new ideas may concern questions of faith, or doubts he has had in the past or perhaps even doubts he has never had. The study may have an impact on his situation at home or at work, or on his understanding of the Church; the problem might be celibacy and marriage, finance or anything else. New insights can awaken hidden concerns about authority, obedience, loyalty or personal relationships. I could give concrete examples of each and every one.

In itself a crisis can be a good thing. A crisis is a point in time when dormant questions come to the surface and must be addressed. An internal conflict is a fight between two or more points of view or interest in the person. Issues need to be clarified, choices must be made. All this is a matter of healthy growth. A crisis is painful; it can produce panic. Forces which feel out of control awaken emotions that have remained out of awareness and that now rise to the surface and compete with each other. A man may not even be able to give a name to these unknown motivations and this can be distinctly unsettling. He does not understand what is happening and he fears that he is losing control. He tries to calm down, but in vain. He does not understand what has happened. Call it chaos, panic or crisis.

Some people are control freaks: they always have to be in charge of themselves. It is exactly this kind of person who is most likely to be thrown by the unknown. They are less able to cope with a crisis. Many candidates who come forward for service in the Church acknowledge that they feel the need for certainty and control. It is clearly important that people who are called to leadership should be confident of themselves, at ease in a clear framework of truths and values. But leaders are also the people who are most vulnerable to inner crises!

Quite a few candidates would prefer to prepare for ordination at a secular institute where they can pick and choose and do not have to fit into an established structure where everything is determined by the Church. This is not meant to be a judgment. We try only to observe what goes on in people even if they are not aware of it themselves. We do not doubt the sincerity of such convictions, nor the principles and values held by such people. It is not our intention to challenge what they say and do just for the sake of challenging. But priestly formation must help people resolve and deal with their major inner conflicts so that what they want to be will not be too strongly contradicted by inner struggles that have been left untouched and that could seriously damage their work.

A crisis resembles growing pain. Personalities do not grow in straight lines but in a kind of a spiral. Children do not go straight from one stage to the next. Before finally moving into the next stage of development they often appear to regress, falling back into an earlier phase, only then to jump on to the next. Personal development often follows a pattern of one step back and two steps forward. Older men are just as likely as younger candidates to regress as conflicts, anxieties, uncertainties and defence mechanisms are reactivated, especially when they have never been properly recognized or addressed in the past.

The crises that candidates can go through are not only intellectual, spiritual or practical. They can be psychological as well. It is sometimes difficult to separate out the different levels and see what has triggered the crisis, or understand how the different levels interact with each other as the crisis unfolds. But levels of being cannot be neatly compartmentalized. Moreover, intellectual, personal and spiritual levels of experience can, and do, interact in unexpected ways. What matters is whether the person has the spiritual resources of an authentic faith to cope with the inevitable limitations of the human condition, including those crises which are a normal part of growing up. Can he recognise and accept the demands of a crisis? Can he consider these inner forces with equanimity and integrate them into his true self?

It goes without saying that a man going through a crisis or conflict may need to be accompanied by someone else, someone who understands what is going on. This is where the Spiritual Director plays a critical role. He must help the candidate to see God's hand at work in this turmoil. In some cases it may be necessary to get professional help from a supervisor, a psychologist or a psychiatrist as well. It is important to get to the bottom of the matter as far as possible – to clarify the issues, explore the roots, the intensity and the strength of the feelings, and consider what consequences all of this might have on the candidate's daily life.

Nobody worries if a fuse occasionally blows at home, but when power failures start to become routine then it is time to call an electrician. The expert must then investigate – was this an accidental overload or a sign of some deeper structural problem? Many things in life can be put right. If one of the faculty has little training in the human sciences he may get worried about longer lasting consequences if he notices a man getting unduly stressed, and might even start to have doubts about that person's suitability for holy orders. It may sound odd (though probably not) that it is often precisely the model student who caused little anxiety during training who struggles more after ordination than other students who worked through some of these issues during formation. The advantage of having one's problems addressed during training is that more often than not they can be dealt with.

Having said that, it can happen that faculty members start to feel uneasy about a candidate during training because the student appears to suffer from serious inner conflicts, a situation which is likely sooner or later get that person into serious difficulty. On the surface, it can appear that there is nothing wrong, but this is where tutors may have to follow their own intuition and try to get the devil out into the open. The old seminaries and novitiates worked that way, although it was not clear that they always had the staff with the necessary counselling skills required to guide the man through.

This is why Bovendonk has a system of mentoring. During the last two years of training students are formed into small groups, each of which is given a supervisor. At an earlier stage, during the first two years each student has a mentor they are advised to see at every residential weekend. We are lucky enough to be able to draw on a number of women religious who have training and experience in spirituality and psychology to help in this way, and these mentors work with students as part of their own ministry. This relationship can be continued after the first two years if the student so wishes. These meetings fall under the umbrella of the so-called *forum internum,* which means they are strictly confidential. The mentor may advise a student to take up an issue with the Rector, the Spiritual Director or a staff member, but it is entirely up to the student to accept this advice or not.

Fear of being dismissed

For a few students there is always the fear of being asked to leave. A little strange perhaps for adults; ideally one would hope that they would see Bovendonk as an opportunity to explore their vocation and move towards a mature decision. If they could see it that way, then perhaps they could start to see the Rector and faculty as helpers and guides. But in practice, there are always a handful of students who see the faculty as judge and jury, always on the look-out for reasons to prevent them from achieving the goal of ordination. As if the staff would want anything other than to insure that as many students as possible would become good priests and deacons!

It reminds me of one student many years ago, who had held a senior position in his previous secular employment and yet was so suspicious of me that one day I found myself saying: 'after all these years, it looks as if you are still afraid of me!' 'Yes', he said, 'of course I am! Until you sign the final recommendation there is no guarantee that I shall be ordained. That is the way it works.' Perhaps, who knows, that says more about me than him.

Perhaps I am only reflecting my own training at the Institute for Psychology in Rome. That institute is very demanding. Most of the students are either priests or members of religious orders and the institute deliberately sets out to create high levels of anxiety. Fear of failure or of being dismissed was not an issue, though. I find it easier to understand that the younger students might feel like that, but not the older ones.

The first of the eight basic conflicts Erikson claims each person has to negotiate is that of trust versus distrust. This springs from experience in the first year of life. The infant has to develop a basic trust in the world around him. To what extent is life safe and predictable? Erikson argues that infants who are cared for by a moody and sullen person develop an attitude of distrust which then affects the way they relate to other people throughout their lives. For such people, all authority -superiors or institutes - are bossy, untrustworthy and unpredictable. Anybody can be deceived or betrayed in later life, but for people who have formed this kind of orientation this only confirms what they already feel.

We are not talking about children who have been abused. That too will influence later life, but in different ways. But apart from such cases - exceptional ones we hope - there are students who constantly run up against people of authority in the Church and elsewhere. They need to get to grips with the hidden conflict that disturbs them. It may be a good thing therefore that there is at least one staff member they find difficult. Conflicts will bring these feelings to the surface so that students can start to learn to cope with them. Without such conflict, the problem may remain deeply buried.

A life of regular prayer

One of the greatest challenges facing students whose training is done in part-time mode, as at Bovendonk, is the development of a rhythm and discipline in daily life that makes it possible to find space for a regular prayer life. This is more than an issue of time. This is undoubtedly easier to organise in a residential seminary, though this does not mean that the seminarian who has attended regular times of prayer and meditation for years will necessarily have internalized the practise sufficiently to continue after ordination. I hear students complaining all the time that it is almost impossible to fit in fixed times for prayer in their busy work schedule. They count themselves lucky if they can find one brief slot each day to pray. It helps to discuss this issue with a Spiritual Director.

It is good for them to understand that they will encounter precisely the same difficulty of establishing a regular prayer life after ordination when they will be overburdened with the pastoral work and management tasks of a parochial minister. In a certain sense, the life of a part-time student resembles that of the full time priest or deacon more than the regular routine found in traditional seminaries.

What has struck me is that, apart from the organized retreats and Quiet Days at Bovendonk, many students will increasingly take the initiative to spend a weekend or a whole week in a monastery or a convent to go into retreat. Once they have given up their secular employment and gone into a full-time pastoral placement, their prayer life often improves notably. It would be worthwhile to research of the pattern of spirituality found amongst diocesan clergy and try to correlate this to the type of training programme (seminary or other) he attended. But that calls for another book!

Preparing for the pastoral placement

Priestly formation is unthinkable these days without a period of practical pastoral experience. It is important, however, to prepare for it. Halfway through the fourth year, the student puts forward a proposal for a parish placement. This is an important step even if he has been looking forward to it throughout the first four years of training. It is a watershed moment, complete with risk and challenge. It means resigning from his existing job, a very public act, set down in writing, and from which there is often no way back. It may mean moving house. It means giving up the familiar and secure world in which he has lived. It means stepping out into the unknown with all the insecurity that involves. A candidate who used to be a schoolteacher once said to me: I have known no other world than the school. First as a pupil, then as a teacher. Every hour of the day, the week, the year was been scheduled. Everything in his work was predictable and planned.

If they own a property, students are always advised to hang on to it. Some students sell because they are required to move into diocesan accommodations to live in community with other seminarians of that diocese. I have questioned the diocesan Rectors about this several times, but they will not change their minds. Students accept the fact passively, but in some cases with a degree of resentment or even passive aggression.

I can also see the positive side of this 'community life' during the two years of pastoral experience, particularly so when students live in the same house as the parish priest. There they can learn about the daily life of a priest as they pray, work, eat together. The student has time to reflect and to ask questions to the senior priest who is always his first guide and mentor for the practical placement. In any case, 'Bovendonk' requires the student at least to live within the boundaries of the placement parish in order to be a member of the community of faith.

Those who own their own business may have to sell it, or at least relinquish their share of it. Friends or colleagues who may have applauded the initial decision to train for the priesthood may now express disapproval. They may regret losing a valued colleague. Students can come under considerable pressure and the faculty must show understanding of the problems this may present.

Students understandably want to understand the practical arrangements as fully as possible before they make the final decision. Where will the diocese put them, who will be their supervisor, and what will they be like? What will be the arrangements for theological reflection, and what is the system for supervision? What about pensions and insurance? The fourth year is a time of momentous change for students. The first steps in planning will be made with the student's Spiritual Director, but there will also be meetings with those responsible for pastoral placements in each diocese, and with the placement supervisor and the lecturer of pastoral theology. Another important meeting is with the diocesan treasurer to organise the financial arrangements for the placement. And there may be many other things to be organized as well.

The end of the initial formation process

Initial training normally comes to an end after six years, when the student finishes his pastoral placement and is ordained. Six out of ten of the students starting at Bovendonk reach this goal. Personally I think that losing four out of ten students is still rather high, but it is 10 % below the average for seminaries. Perhaps the 'drop-out' rate is lower because of the stricter selection process at Bovendonk.

As I have already said, with the benefit of hindsight I must admit, a few people were allowed to start training even though I had some doubt initially about their suitability. In some cases, the selection process was unduly fore-shortened, as happened when an application was made shortly before the start of the academic year. I admit that I have gone ahead and allowed some to start every so often because other colleagues took a more positive view of the prospective student. It has also happened that in spite of obvious unresolved conflict in a person, I felt, despite my better judgment and against all I had been taught, that the person should be offered a chance. In some cases I judged wrongly. We have sometimes asked ourselves - I mean my colleagues and I - why we allowed this to happen.

Our students may not agree, but at times I think the answer is that we were simply too trusting. We thought the individual concerned would grow out of his problems once he had been ordained. Strictly speaking, one should only admit older candidates for training if they are clearly ready for ordination in terms of faith, personal maturity and self-awareness, and lack only theological knowledge or practical pastoral 'know-how'. This should clearly be the case for permanent deacons, and maybe also for priests, if the so-called *viri probati* are allowed to be ordained.

Today's world is becoming more and more complex. As a result, it is also becoming more and more difficult for a training programme to give candidates all the psycho-spiritual resources needed to cope. This means taking risks - responsible levels of risk to be sure, but risk nonetheless. Risk of disappointment for a student who started full of hope and courage and risk of disappointment for the faculty member as well who stuck out his neck to admit a candidate whom he thought could succeed and whom he hoped to have as a colleague one day. All we can do is seek to minimize the risk and in that way limit the number of disappointments.

It is always painful when a student has to give up training after he has started. This is true not only for the student but for the faculty as well, especially if they had high hopes for the candidate. It is always something the staff have to approach with considerable caution, and I think I can honestly say this has nearly always been the case. It is important that those responsible for formation can say exactly why they decided training has to be terminated. What concrete evidence can they give that suggests this is the proper outcome?

It will not do simply to say 'you are not suitable', or 'you are better off remaining as a layman in the Church'. It sometimes happens that the staff start to feel that all is not right with a particular candidate, but they cannot say why. It is all a matter of a vague feeling, intuitions which are hard to put into words. In minor seminaries it was customary to say in such cases 'why not continue your education in a secular school and get some experience of ordinary life; then, if you want to come back in a few years time, let us know', hoping, of course, that the student will never come back! If he did return, you had a problem, for you could not easily go back on your word.

In any case, with adult men this simply will not do. It is not right. Adults deserve better treatment when they are trying to work through questions which have been with them for years. They did not start walking the road to the priesthood lightly. They will have most likely thought about it for years before even taking the first step. Am I suitable or not? They will have struggled with the question. They have been accepted, and they have started the training. If it has to be stopped, they are entitled to an honest explanation.

Students who make their own decision to withdraw present different problems. Some are quite determined. They simply let you know their decision and disappear, sometimes too quickly in my opinion. From their point of view there is nothing further to decide, they have made a decision. Others are forced to give up because of financial problems that even the diocese cannot help resolve, or because of home situation has changed or for health reasons. This is always tough. They have to give up a future which they believed was really right for them.

But in the majority of cases, the students concerned have come to realize over time that ordination is not the right way forward, but they needed time to work this through: the heart understands, but the head needs to be convinced. The Rector often recognizes the early symptoms: they start to miss weekends for no obvious reason, they ask for time-off, or they make impossible conditions about the choice of pastoral placement (in the hope somebody else will make the decision for them). You tolerate their behaviour in order to allow them to leave honourably. They have not been dismissed and – in their own minds – they have not been forced into a decision or felt the need to explain it to others.

This is the student who disappears from the scene without taking leave of his fellow students. They just leave things unclear and leave with: 'I shall be in touch with you in a year or so' although you know they will not. If the hesitation lasts too long the Rector has to intervene and help the student to see that he has in fact already made up his mind but lacks the courage to face it. Looking back later, they usually recognize that they were grateful for the help you gave them.

Ideal, fantasy and reality

Having reread again my account of Bovendonk triggers the question: why did I write any of this? A colleague who read an earlier draft focused the point sharply when he said 'for whom are you writing this?' For future students? For those involved in formation?' I thought it was a good question. Does everything have to be published? And why not? What will readers make of it? Does it give a balanced account of Bovendonk? Will it help any future students or will it hinder them? The more I thought about it, the more questions arose. Fortunately there were a few wise people who were willing not only to read my text but also to allow me to ask my questions.

I came to the conclusion that what I really wanted to do is to give an account of my experience and of the way in which I arrived at the many decisions that had to be made. What have I learned from all these years as Rector? What practical day–to-day decisions did I make, and why? More than anything else I wanted to pass on some of my experience to my successors, to those who might be involved elsewhere in the formation of older candidates for the priesthood and the diaconate, and to those who might participate in a training programme like Bovendonk, in the hope that it might be of some help to them.

One colleague who has played a major role in setting up the programme for deacons suggested that in fact I had given my readers the opportunity to look into the kitchen, that is to say to give a glimpse of what goes on behind the scenes. And in so doing, I had, of course, made myself vulnerable. Some people, he said, will not like what has been written. They prefer to hold on to an idealized picture. He could be right.

Despite all the evidence to the contrary, we often try to hold on to an ideal image of the perfect system full of people without any shortcomings or limitations. Some people do. This romantic image makes priests and religious into people who are never annoyed or impatient, always kind and joyful, always wise. Such an impossible ideal denies the reality of the human condition and borders on pure fantasy. As we saw in an earlier chapter, the Self consists of many layers in which the ideal self and the real self are quite distinct. The more we disapprove of the real Self the more we risk raising the bar. We set higher, stricter and unrealistic standards for ourselves and for everyone around us.

The gap between ideal and reality grows bigger and we become ever more frustrated at our own failure to live up to our own ideals. The end result is a humourless and unpleasant personality. Such impossible demands can lead to spiritual despair as well as stress-related physical disorders. Following Jesus Christ is a high ideal, but it is also a realistic ideal. This is something we must never forget and which needs to be publically proclaimed. Ideals can only be reached by the grace of God and with our human co-operation. People before us have managed to find the proper way forward – it is called holiness. But it does not make sense to pretend we have reached such a state, if in reality we have hardly recognized the problem.

One of my teachers used to say 'People like to think their lives are like driving a new luxury car along a perfect highway, when in fact it is more like riding a tractor over bumpy roads.' The Lord gives us an entire lifetime to work at our sanctification, a whole life to strive for the ideal step-by-step; two forwards, one backwards. The starting point is always the reality of the way we are, not what we would like to be. If we overlook this simple fact of life, we are chasing an illusion. Instead, let us learn to accept the human condition and everything it implies, joyfully, gratefully, humbly.

This dynamic operates, not only at the level of each individual person but at community level, in local Churches as well as the Church at large. It is good to have high ideals, but we must remain realistic and honest. If people fail to take proper account of human nature and the realities of life and church governance is organised solely around unrealistic ideals, then frustration is inevitable. The gap between ideal and reality becomes unbridgeable and people simply drop out. What other choice do they have but either to pull out or put up with a permanent contradiction between reality and ideal? From their own experience the ideal is unreachable.

Children in particular can become enormously frustrated by parents who are always right, who cannot be vulnerable, and who always present their perfect side. They are always right, full stop. Such parents often impose the same perfectionism on the children, who cannot reach it either, but quickly learns to pretend. These children learn to internalize a debilitating sense of inadequacy because they know they can never measure up to what their parents expect of them. Some students may feel the same in relation to demands made by the way an Institute presents itself; as perfect.

It is good to give children high ideals, things worth working for. But at the same time they also need to learn to live with their own limitations, accept there are some things they will never be able to achieve. 'Perfect' parents make it impossible for children to learn to live appropriately with their own inadequacies and failings. Mistakes or problems can never be acknowledged because my parents are big, perfect and immune, and I am small, incapable and always wrong. I am a permanent failure.

As soon as this child grows up and discovers that he is not an idiot, that sometimes he does get it right and that others have played games with him, he will step out of the game and rebel. Most of them anyway. From that moment on, he will not take other people seriously unless that other person is capable of being honest about his doubts and limitations, and allows his vulnerability to show. Only then will he take the other person seriously. Unfortunately, it also happens that some people have internalized the perfect parent model so successfully that they can no longer detach themselves from it. They become a clone of their perfect parents. Sadly, this is true even among priests or deacons.

If the Almighty accepts and respects the laws that govern human behaviour that He Himself has created, then it might seem a little odd if we do not. In the formation of priests and deacons I have made an effort to get the students to discover, to accept, and even to love, the limitations of the Church and their own. They are not perfect; rather they are ordinary human beings with a deep and sincere faith they want to share with others and that they, as priests and spiritual leaders, 'carriers of the Mystery', want to model for others.

9. LATE VOCATION: A PERSONAL REFLECTION[70]

By Han van den Blink

Introduction

I have called this lecture *Late Vocation: A Personal Reflection*. Mine is a late priestly vocation. I was 59 years old when I was ordained to the Anglican priesthood, more than thirty years after I was ordained in the Presbyterian Church. Before being priested, I spent most of my professional life as a pastoral counsellor and psychologist. In retrospect, I can see that what led to my feeling called to the priesthood had been going on long before I became fully aware of it. I know that this is the experience of many. It was as if, after a number of years, several underground streams merged together and burst to the surface of my awareness.

Never in my wildest dreams would I have imagined myself as a priest and never would I have been able to predict that I would spend the remaining years of my career teaching ascetical and pastoral theology in a seminary. Neither would I have ever been able to anticipate how profoundly right it would feel to be a priest and to know in my heart that this is what I am called to be. When Matt Ham asked me to share with you on this festive day a personal reflection on my experience of becoming a priest later in life, I was both greatly honoured by his invitation and sufficiently intrigued to accept. I have taken seriously, as you will discover, Matt's request to make this a personal reflection.

When I thought of how to structure this lecture, I recalled the two aspects of my experience, both in the process of seeking ordination and afterwards, that were most critical in pulling the varied pieces of my life together and contributing decisively to my own spiritual formation. These two aspects are a renewed understanding of the traditional notion of *purgation* and the desire

---

[70]After living abroad for more than four decades, it is easier for me to write in English as I discovered when I attempted to compose this lecture in Dutch. For that reason I am especially grateful to Drs. A. G. A. van Heeswijk for providing the Dutch translation and to Dr. J. H. N. Kerssemakers for his support. Both Ad and Jacques are psychologists and active in the KSGV (Katholiek Studiecentrum voor Geestelijke Volksgezondheid). Ad is a member of its Redactiecommissie and Jacques is its Studiesecretaris.

to allow this understanding to shape my behaviour during difficult times, and discovering how critically important the regular cultivation of *hesychia* is for such a process of integration.

The Greek word *hesychia*, meaning silence and quietude, was much beloved by the Fathers of the early Church. I have chosen to use it because it is a word rich in meaning, describing not just absence of sound and physical stillness, but inner quietude, equanimity and tranquillity and, most important of all, openness to the presence of the Holy Spirit. The *hesychast* tradition is an active spiritual practice which has traditionally centred on the use of the Jesus Prayer, "Lord Jesus Christ, Son of God, have mercy on me a sinner", as a way of being still and knowing God.[71]

Accustomed as I was as a psychologist to think of the process of personal integration in psychological terms, it surprised me to realize that neither psychological insight nor psychotherapy but spiritual formation provided the means for this to happen. Although the choice of *purgation* and *hesychia* is personal, I know from my experience with deacons and priests who have trusted me with their stories that *purgation* and *hesychia* also can play an integrative role in the lives of others.

Before I proceed any further, I want those of you in this audience who are deacons or are in training for ordination to the permanent diaconate to know that everything I have to say today about priestly spiritual formation applies to you as well.

In preparing for this lecture I began by asking several Anglican and Roman Catholic priests about their thoughts on late vocations to the priesthood.[72] I know these men well and respect their judgment. I got some interesting answers. One, a seminary Dean, told me that although he knew a few success cases, his general impression of late vocations was not particularly positive. When I asked him to explain, he said that in his experience older candidates for ordination, those in their 40's and 50's, are less malleable and open to change and, therefore, less likely to benefit from the formation process during their time in seminary.

---

[71]cf. Psalm 46:10. For an excellent introduction to the Jesus Prayer, see Bishop Kallistos Ware, *The Power of the Name: The Jesus Prayer in Orthodox Spirituality* (SLG Press, Fairacres Publication 43, 1996).

[72]These priests are (in alphabetical order): the Very Rev. Martin Boler, OSB, the Rev. Dr. John A. Colacino, C.PP.S, the Rev. Canon Carl Gerdau, the Very Rev. Dr. John R. Kevern, and the Rt. Rev. Kenneth Price.

He found that many are looking for ordination to solve personal problems or to achieve a measure of self-actualization that had escaped them elsewhere. Another drawback he mentioned was that many older candidates for ordination are imbued with a modernist or even post-modernist mindset. Such a mindset, inevitably internalized by those of us born in Western Europe and North America, is characterized by an uncritical assent to the truth of prevailing secular views about the nature of reality. This mindset, as I will explain later, can constitute a major obstacle to spiritual formation.

In answer to the same question, an older priest's immediate response was that some of the late vocations he knew were the best and some were the worst that he had encountered. This particular priest has for a number of years occupied a position of major responsibility in the Episcopal Church, as the Anglican Church is called in the US. For this reason he has been in a position to observe the ministries of many priests. What did the worst have in common I asked? They were escaping, he answered without hesitation. In other words, they were turning to ordination in the hope of finding in the priesthood an answer to whatever was their predicament.

The Prior of a Benedictine Monastery near where I live is usually willing to consider late vocations to monastic life, some of them already ordained men themselves. He has, however, run into the same problem that the seminary Dean referred to, namely that these candidates are often more set in their ways than is desirable for monastic life and frequently have too many unresolved personal problems to make them suitable for acceptance into the novitiate. The Prior also emphasized that acculturation takes more time for those who are older. A similar view was expressed by a Roman Catholic priest who had been Director of Formation in his own congregation.

An Episcopal Bishop with long experience in Diocesan leadership had a more positive view. He told me that he is a strong supporter of late vocations, even for those in their 60s and 70s. He traced this appreciation of late vocations back to being asked at one point in his ministry to design and then run a part-time Diocesan program of academic and spiritual formation for those who were called to the priesthood later in life and who were for a variety of reasons not able to attend a regular seminary.

Rather than underperforming, as was confidently expected by many, these candidates for ordination did better in the final examination of the seven canonical areas[73] that is required of all candidates for ordination in the Episcopal Church than those who had obtained their theological degrees in a regular seminary. He also stressed that all those who had gone through that program were highly motivated and that those who were still alive were flourishing in the priesthood.

What did these late vocations have in common I asked? The first thing the Bishop mentioned was that before being ordained, they invariably had been successful in their careers, such as running a department store, owning a bakery, working as an engineer, a social worker or an executive in a steel company.

This observation was echoed by a Roman Catholic priest who wrote that older candidates for ordination at the Sacred Heart School of Theology in Hales Corners, Wisconsin were men who usually had successful secular careers including "doctors, lawyers, bankers, engineers, teachers, architects, accountants, employees of the FBI, military officers, commercial pilots, construction workers, carpenters, and farmers." but who became "convinced that there ought to be more to life than the accumulation of wealth and the attainment of a prestigious position in society."[74] He also mentioned that widowed men were frequently among candidates for ordination.

Were there other factors that contributed to their being successful priests I asked the Episcopal Bishop? Yes, there were, and he mentioned four of them. First, every one of these candidates was carefully vetted by the Commission on Ministry of the Diocese. Second, they were commonly more spiritually mature than younger candidates and had paid more attention to their spiritual development prior to being considered for ordination. Third, they generally maintained a full devotional life before entering the Diocesan program and were active in their respective parishes. And fourth, they sought to be ordained in response to a strongly felt call from God, not as another career choice but because they felt deeply that something was missing in their lives.

---

[73]This examination, known as the General Ordination Examination, covers the seven canonical areas: Bible, Church History, Theology, Ethics, Liturgics and Church Music, Ascetical and Pastoral Theology.

Adding to what the Bishop said, there is another positive side to late vocations that needs to be highlighted. A common problem among those who are ordained earlier in life is the mistaken assumption that they have achieved a level of personal and spiritual maturity that may not be based in reality. I was struck with what my colleague John Colacino said about this recently, "There is something about church culture that inhibits potential for growth in priests because they all too easily appear, to themselves and others, as finished products. Later vocations may not face this pitfall in the same way if they are developmentally on track and have dealt with some of the challenges of life in a more conducive milieu. If the seminary experience contributes to a deepening and refining of a maturity already there, then such priests may prove to be among the best."[75]

Did these successful late vocations experience any particular problems I asked the Bishop? Yes, he said that they often felt like second class citizens who were looked down on by priests who had gone the regular seminary route. Their lack of experience with a nurturing community of faith also could contribute to spiritual dryness once they were out in the field. Many of them were anxious about being able to meet the academic requirements since they had been out of school for so long. And then there was the factor of lack of support from their families. For those who were married, the call to the priesthood and the change in life style that this would require often caused major conflict with spouses who were settled in their own careers and who did not look kindly on losing their jobs, living on lowered income, or having to move elsewhere.

I was fascinated by the Bishop's account, because it reminded me of what had impressed me during my first visit to *Bovendonk*. In the fall of 2000, John Kevern, the Dean of Bexley Hall Seminary, ran across Matt Ham's article about Bovendonk in *The Tablet*, the International Catholic Weekly. The caption above that article read, "A new sort of seminary has proved a success in the Netherlands. Its students can train part-time for the priesthood while keeping secular jobs or living in religious communities. Its Rector says the results speak for themselves."[76] Since John

---

[75]The Rev. Dr. John A. Colacino, C.PP.S., private communication (used with permission).

Kevern knew that I regularly visit family and friends in the Netherlands, he suggested that I might include a visit to Bovendonk on one of my next trips. As it happened, I was scheduled for a sabbatical leave the very next semester, and so I was privileged, thanks to Matt's hospitality, to spend a weekend at Bovendonk in March 2001.[77]

I found four things here at Bovendonk particularly impressive. First, that students are carefully selected, are expected to succeed, and are given all the help needed to complete their years of study and formation successfully. This makes for a positive and supportive learning environment. Two, that they are held to a high academic standard. This includes being exposed not only to the traditional theological disciplines but also to human sciences that are particularly relevant to pastoral ministry. Third that they receive all the way through their six years in the program, personal mentoring, guidance, and supervision of their pastoral work from experienced men and women. The very length of the Bovendonk program struck me as an advantage. Formation takes time and the three years of full time course work that are required in residential seminaries to complete a Master of Divinity in the US and Canada are hardly sufficient to accomplish adequate formation. And last but not least, it impressed me that regular participation in a Eucharistic community of prayer and worship is foundational to the Bovendonk experience. Bovendonk provides a model for dealing with late vocations in a way that addresses many of the problems that were mentioned in the conversations that I had with my priest colleagues.

It simply is not possible, it would appear, to go through the six years of study and training here without a degree of personal transformation, such as being more aware of one's own

---

[76]Matthias Ham, *Seminary Extraordinary*, *The Tablet*, 21 October 2000, p. 1412.

[77]Like Bovendonk, Bexley is committed to making part-time, non-residential theological education available to those who cannot afford to take off the required time to complete their training in a residential seminary. One of Bexley's challenges in devising its curriculum for part-time and non-residential students was how to maintain the integrity of traditional academic disciplines in tandem with a program of spiritual formation that is more than window dressing. I was eager to see how this challenge was handled at Bovendonk. For more information about Bexley Hall Seminary, I refer the reader to its website: www.bexley.edu.anglican.org

strengths and weaknesses, gaining a deeper understanding of the complexity of human behaviour, a firmer sense of one's pastoral identity, a greater appreciation for the importance of collegiality in ministry, and most important of all, a deeper grounding in matters of the Spirit through prayer, worship, spiritual direction, and theological reflection on a regular basis in the context of a sacramental community. It is no wonder that the graduates of this program are doing so well.

Purgation and *Hesychia*

It has been critically important in my own formation as a priest to be able to understand difficult periods in my life as times of purgation. It is all too easy to misread what is going on at such moments, especially when we believe in the cultural myth of inevitable progress or fall back on standard psychological ways of assessing our predicaments. Since avoiding hard times is not an option, it is essential to appreciate the role that purgation can play in our spiritual formation.

Purgation is one of the three phases or patterns that the Christian tradition, from as far back as the 4th century, has understood as basic to spiritual development. The other two are illumination and union[78]. Looking at my own formation from the perspective of these three has been very helpful to me. We do not, of course, progress routinely and in a direct line from illumination to purgation to union. Indeed, these stages are not discreet, but intermingled, as I have discovered when experiencing God's grace unexpectedly at very difficult moments in my life. They also repeat themselves throughout our life. Purgation, as I learned to my dismay, can appear all too soon on the heels of illumination.

The other important challenge to priestly formation that I want to look at briefly is the practice of *hesychia*. Unlike purgation, however, we can avoid cultivating *hesychia*, we can refrain from prayerfully practicing outer and inner quietude and openness to the Holy Spirit. As a matter of fact, anyone who has tried to cultivate *hesychia* knows that as soon as we set our minds on doing so, all manner of detractions immediately appear to derail

---

[78] I am indebted to the Rev. Dr. John A. Colacino, C.PP.S. for helpful historical information and theological insight regarding the three-fold path of illumination, purgation and union.

our efforts. To avoid this practice, however, is to deprive priesthood of its surest foundation, the experience of God in the here and now of our lives.

First, *purgation.* Why is it so important to understand and respond to difficult times from the perspective of purgation? To begin with, as I have already mentioned, it is very easy to misread this phase of our spiritual journey as failure on our part or a misreading of our calling to the priesthood. Since I am one who has been a firm believer in the myth of progress, seeing the juxtaposition of Jesus' baptism and temptations in the wilderness has served as a paradigm in this regard. Following our Lord's baptism in the Jordan, surely one of the pivotal moments of illumination in his life when the Spirit of God descended on him and he heard a voice from heaven saying, "This is my Son, the Beloved with whom I am well pleased"[79], we are told that he was immediately led by that same Spirit into the wilderness to be tempted by the devil. After the baptism in the Jordan, the desert. After illumination, purgation.

Times of purgation can last for a few hours to weeks or even longer. This can easily throw us for a loop. It is never easy to find oneself in the desert. When I think back on recent times of purgation in my life, I recall the usual moments of feeling down, empty, fatigued, conflicted, being disappointed, or worried. There were also two periods that were much more stressful. The first had to do with being accused falsely and publicly by a colleague of something I had not done. The other was set off by the attacks of September 11, 2001 that reactivated traumatic memories from the Second World War.

Theological students often go through times of purgation while in seminary. For others it happens once they are out, following ordination, in their first parishes or assignments. Major crises and traumas in one's life can also function as times of purgation that, quite unexpectedly, can lead to becoming aware of one's religious vocation. As a matter of fact, that was my own experience. A massive reactivation in the summer of 1988 of trauma I had experienced as a young boy in a Japanese concentration camp at the end of the Second World War set in motion an internal process that led, not many years later, to my seeking ordination. This reactivation, although painful at the time,

---

[79]Matthew 3:17

freed me from habitual ways of remembering and perceiving. It made me aware of the presence of the Spirit during particularly difficult periods, times that I had not forgotten but was not used to looking at through the eyes of faith[80].

Times of purgation, then, are experiences of being in the desert, of being thrown back on oneself, of being thrown off balance, of being disoriented and losing one's footing, of being filled with self-doubt, or of being assaulted by self-denigrating, seductive, humiliating, vengeful, sabotaging ideas and sensations, by what are known in the Eastern Church as *logismoi*,[81] intrusive thoughts and feelings that assault us incessantly, that plague us like a swarm of bees.

We tend to forget that traditionally purgative experiences were understood not in the first place as divine punishment but as invitations to spiritual cleansing, to shedding, as best we can, all that keeps us from being open to the presence of the Holy Spirit, ridding ourselves of all that gets in the way of our awareness of God. Contrary to what we may have been led to believe, such obstacles are not only the obvious sins, such as lying, badmouthing, cheating, stealing, or doing physical, emotional and spiritual harm. They can be, and often are, activities and interests that we consider good. For even at our best, we are limited and fallen creatures who frequently, despite our best intentions, miss the mark.

Understanding this made me appreciate anew the literal meaning of the verb "to sin" in the New Testament, *hamartano*, which means "to miss the mark". It made me see how many times I miss the mark even with the best of intentions. This exegetical clarification of *hamartano* became one of those "Aha!" experiences for me. For it is not only when we do bad things that we miss the mark. We miss the mark just as often when we believe that we are doing good. It is, in other words, not only bad people who are sinners but good people as well. Understanding

---

[80]For a description and analysis of this experience I refer the reader to my article *Trauma Reactivation in Pastoral Counseling*, in *American Journal of Pastoral Counseling*, Vol. 1(2) 1998, pp. 23-39. See also Chapter 3 *De reactivering van trauma's in pastorale counseling: Implicaties voor theorie en praktijk* in my *Pastorale Counseling en Spiritualiteit: Een contextuele benadering*, translated by Ad van Heeswijk (KSGV, Tilburg, 2002).

this can save us from the pernicious moralism that is so pervasive in Christianity.

Purgation, then, not as punishment but as an invitation to *metanoia* ("change of mind") that is to say to turning away from all that hinders our becoming more open to the Holy Spirit and thereby becoming the human beings we are created to be. I cannot overemphasize the importance of this ancient but to me new knowledge. Growing up I learned to understand sin as transgression, as committing acts that are bad, illegal, or immoral. This new understanding of purgation has had much to do with my willingness and ability to live into, and through, trying times differently.

The frequency of these desert experiences makes the availability of regular mentoring, spiritual direction, and trusted colleagues an absolute necessity both for seminarians and for priests. The availability of spiritual direction and regular mentoring is critical to the health of the Church's ministry and, where I live and work, greatly needed and widely neglected. I have been enormously helped by the mentoring and spiritual direction I have received. And I have found that trusted colleagues are indispensable to ministry.

Insights from the human sciences can, of course, also be very helpful. We need to have as thorough an understanding as we can muster of the best of the human sciences so that we can use them in our ministry and for our own growth in self-awareness. I heard this same point made by Francis Cline, the Abbott of the Cistercian Monastery in Mepkin, South Carolina. He pointed out that every age makes its particular contribution to the enrichment of the Christian tradition and that a more nuanced understanding of human dynamics is the gift of our own time.[82] One of the important things I have had to learn is to appreciate the insights of psychology, the usefulness of psychotherapy, or, for that matter, the contribution that medications can make in restoring us to a degree of balance and health, without making any of these ends into themselves.

There is another aspect about times of purgation of which that I have become aware. They invariably activate internalized cultural

---

[82]Francis Cline, OCSO, Lecture "On being an Abbott" [audiotape], Mount Saviour Benedictine Monastery, Pine City, New York, 1995.

beliefs about the nature of reality. The two most dominant cultural beliefs that I struggle with are materialism, and by materialism I mean the philosophy and not the desire for material possessions, and with what the philosopher Alasdair MacIntyre has called aptly *emotivism*.[83].

Materialism is the belief that physical processes are the foundation of all of life, including consciousness and religious beliefs. What characterizes materialism most of all is its utter inability to accept the reality of the immaterial. Since matters of the spirit by definition deal with the Immaterial, religious faith is marginalized as insignificant at best or written off as superstition at worst. More people than we realize, including many in the pews and in the clergy, struggle with this issue. People of faith want to believe, but their cultural conditioning makes it often difficult for them to realize that they are looking at the Christian faith through materialist glasses. This makes them easy prey for those who are trying to deconstruct the doctrines of the Christian faith and fashion a non-theistic Christianity in its place.[84]

The other dominant belief in our Western society is *emotivism*, that is to say the assumption that the subjective self is the arbiter of what is good and right and truthful. The prevailing psychological reductionism of this emotivist mindset is evident all around us in the increasing privatization of experience, the belief that the conscious, subjective self in its "thinking, observing, measuring and estimating," and I am quoting Thomas Merton, "is absolutely primary ... [and is] the one indubitable reality [from which] all truth starts."[85]

I have observed this emotivist reductionism in seminary students, faculty, clergy, and more often than I would like to admit, also in myself. I happened on a classic example of this mindset one day in a seminary corridor when I walked by two students who were

---

[83] Alasdair MacIntyre, *After Virtue: A Study in Moral Theory*, Second Edition (University of Notre Dame Press, 1984), pp19-22

[84] The retired Episcopal Bishop John Shelby Spong and the Cambridge theologian Don Cupitt are leaders in this movement. Representative of their writings are Spong's *Christianity must Change or Die* (HarperSanFrancisco, 1998) and Cupitt's *After God* (Weidenfeld and Nicolson, 1997). An article by the feminist theologian Manuela Kalsky in a recent issue of *Volzin*, "Ik wil graag dat God ongrijpbaar blijft", espouses a similar viewpoint (25 July, 2003, pp. 6-9).

[85] Thomas Merton, *Zen and the Birds of Appetite*, (New Directions Press, 1968) p. 22.

engaged in a theological debate. As I walked by, I heard one of them say with great conviction, "I cannot accept that, because it is not my truth." It is the emphasis on my that betrays the emotivist mindset.

My point is that even when we disagree strongly with these dominant cultural beliefs, as I assume most of us here do, they remain powerful shapers of our behavior, as I discovered, precisely because they are internalized. It is easy to forget that our vocations always take place in a specific cultural context and that this context profoundly influences and shapes us in all that we do, including our religious vocations. Pope John Paul II made the same point when he wrote, "God always calls his priests from specific human and ecclesial contexts, which inevitably influence them."[86]

To the degree that we are not aware of such internalized cultural beliefs and values, their ability to influence our perceptions and shape our behavior is even greater. Like all values and beliefs we have internalized, they are triggered in times of crisis, in the same manner that our past traumas get reactivated whenever we go through any new upsetting or traumatic experience.[87] We are like fish swimming in the waters of our culture and filtering these same waters through our gills. In other words, we are in the water, but the water is also in us.

Materialism and *emotivism*, once activated, manifest themselves in predictable ways. The first will immediately undermine our faith in what I have referred to as "the reality of the immaterial". This instantly translates in a diminishing of trust in the active presence of God in our lives. For that reason we should not be surprised that even the most faithful priest or deacon can find himself, suddenly and to his own dismay, in a mood of utter agnosticism. Not knowing what causes such a rapid shift in perceptions can occasion a good deal of unnecessary suffering.

---

[86] Pope John Paul II, *Pastores Dabo Vobis: Post-Synodal Apostolic Exhortation on the Formation of Priests in the Circumstances of the Present*, 1992, Chapter 1, No. 5.

[87] *Trauma Reactivation in Pastoral Counseling,* in *American Journal of Pastoral Counseling*, Vol. 1(2) 1998, pp. 23-39. See also Chapter 3 *De reactivering van trauma's in pastorale counseling: Implicaties voor theorie en praktijk* in my *Pastorale Counseling en Spiritualiteit: Een contextuele benadering*, translated by Ad van Heeswijk (KSGV, Tilburg, 2002).

Emotivism only makes things worse by leading us to believe that the way we feel at any given moment is really what is going on. In my work as priest, seminary professor, and Spiritual Director I have had occasion to observe extraordinary emotivist conclusions. One that I have heard many times can be summarized as follows, "When I feel that God is close, then I know that God exists but when I do not feel God's presence, then God does not exist". I trust that the absurdity of this manner of thinking is obvious.

In order to avoid misunderstanding, I need to draw a distinction between different kinds of feelings. As we all know, feelings can be very helpful in telling us what is going on. Feelings can and do play a very important role in discerning the truth. If we think we are alright but our body tells us otherwise, we better pay attention. It can be dangerous to disregard pain or a sense of uneasiness. On more than one occasion my feeling that something was wrong, for instance while driving, has saved me from harm. Feeling that there is something not right about an important relationship can rescue friendships or save marriages that have gone off track. In such cases the opposite is also true, namely that denying such diagnostic feelings can doom marriages and friendships.

Feelings also play an important role in our spiritual journey. In this regard I have learned much from the 4th and 5th century Abbas and Ammas of Egypt, Palestine, and Syria, many of them late vocations themselves. These desert monastics frequently addressed the spiritual importance of feelings, such as our strongly felt desire for God or our tears of *penthos*, that is to say tears of compunction and repentance. To them what marked the authentic saint was this gift of *penthos*, of sorrow over the many times that we miss the mark. "Truly you are blessed, Abba Arsenius," Abba Poemen exclaimed, "for you wept for yourself in this world!"[88]

Tears of *penthos* are tears that flow when, in the presence of God, we are able to drop our mask, when we are able to see ourselves as we really are, when the hardness and the defenses of our hearts are pierced and we glimpse the promise of forgiveness and renewal. These are the tears that signify a

---

[88] Quoted in Irenee Hausherr, SJ, *Penthos: The Doctrine of Compunction in the Christian East* (Cistercian Publications, 1982), p. 1.

broken heart and a greater humility. "Create in me a clean heart, O God, and renew a right spirit within me."[89]

These Abbas and Ammas were not discouraged by sin and failure but always saw it as an opportunity for *metanoia*, for conversion. Theirs was an enormous optimism about the possibility of spiritual change, of making a course correction, of turning toward God. For that reason they were not afraid of sin or of sinners for they had experienced the inexhaustible depth of God's mercy and grace themselves.

The reason I am expanding on this at some length is to stress that I have learned to be careful in discerning what kinds of feelings I am having or dealing with, especially during desert times. Some feelings are helpful, good and even, like *penthos*, spiritual necessities. Others, like those activated in emotivism, can lead us astray. What marks emotivist feelings is that they are what is known as conditioned responses. A feeling of disgust, for instance, that is triggered when confronted by food that we have been taught is unfit for consumption, is a conditioned response.

Such powerful conditioned responses, needless to say, also become attached to cultural beliefs. Late vocations need to be especially aware of this phenomenon. For both materialism and *emotivism* can generate a strong feelings of being right, of possessing the truth. In our culture rigid materialistic views are frequently accompanied by feelings of superiority. This feeling of "being right" is, as you know, commonly paired with a negative critique of religious faith and/or a dismissal of anything that even smells like doctrine. It is not surprising that so many seekers in our time draw a sharp distinction between spirituality which is deemed good and desirable and organized religion which is considered oppressive and restricting. I hear this a lot, and I am sure that you do too.

When students wonder what the relevance of theology is to spirituality, I like to point out that one of the important functions of theology is to serve as a map to let us know when we are off course and as a lens to help us see things of which we would otherwise not be aware. Without a theological perspective, for example, it would be impossible to discern what we are going through as a time of purgation. Without a theological point of view

---

[89] Psalm 51:11.

it would not be possible to see it as a time of cleansing and testing and deepening of one's relation to God rather than as a time of abandonment or confusion.

What I have learned and am learning from this understanding of purgation is that to the person of faith everything that has happened, everything that is now going on, and everything that is yet to come about, whether wonderful and gratifying or traumatic and difficult is an invitation to let go of the ego and become more conscious of our utter dependence on God. "Only when our limits are claimed and acknowledged", wrote one of my students with great insight, echoing the Abbas and Ammas, "can we begin to draw on the unlimited power of God."[90]

Let me repeat that we are not asked to eradicate our egos, as is often believed erroneously, but to de-center them. We need our ego as an administrator of our affairs. We do not need our ego to be the Sovereign of our life. We need our ego for planning. We do not need our ego for trying to control everything and everyone. This is the great blessing that times of purgation can convey. Purgation when responded to in this manner can increase both our self-knowledge, deepen our trust in God and our ability to see whatever transpires *sub specie aeternitatis,* and free us from self-pre-occupation and worry over matters that we cannot control. This was the great strength of so many early Christians and it can be ours as well.

And now to *hesychia*. Why is cultivating *hesychia,* that is to say engaging in regular contemplative prayer so important? Isn't it enough to say one's prayers, observe the daily office, participate faithfully in the Eucharist, and so forth? Why is it important to build into one's schedule a regular time of contemplative prayer, of sitting silently before God, as part of one's spiritual practice? Isn't it, as I have heard said on more than one occasion, only for monastics or for introverts?

The answer to these questions is more complex that might be expected. I have discovered that there are at least four aspects of such a spiritual practice that need to be kept in mind: differentiation from cultural norms, seeking balance, increasing self-awareness, and practicing the presence of God. Let me briefly address each of these in turn.

---

[90]Amy Fauquet, Unpublished paper, May 2003.

First, differentiation from cultural and ecclesial norms and expectations. Ministry is extraordinarily demanding. It has rightly been called the impossible vocation. Being a priest or deacon regularly puts one in the middle of a vortex of opposing and often conflicting demands, needs, expectations, political pressures, and emotional transferences and counter-transferences, to name just a few. On any given day, we can go from the hospital to a baptism, from a funeral to a birthday party, from hearing a confession to mediating a marital conflict, from chairing a parish committee to dealing with the complaints of various parishioners, or trying to resolve a burgeoning political conflict, all the while trying to prepare ourselves to preach and teach, and keep ourselves going by getting a bite to eat on the run.

What complicates all this is a culture which, at least where I live, lives at breakneck speed, is focused on performance and results and on the bottom line, is ignorant and intolerant of the need for authentic *sabbath* time –for many people even vacations have become work-- and does not hold what clergy do in very high regard. Moreover, many clergy are workaholics. We preach peace and we convey the opposite. To cultivate regular times of silence, quiet, and meditation is, therefore, profoundly counter cultural. Cultivating *hesychia* is a challenge for everyone, regardless of age, but is of particular importance, in my experience, for those who are called to the priesthood later in life, precisely because it goes so much against our ingrained habits and cultural conditioning.

Second, seeking balance. In a recent conference on Benedictine spirituality, the Archbishop of Canterbury, Dr. Rowan Williams, gave an address on the implications for our time of St. Benedict's *Regula*.[91] He pointed out that the holiness Benedict envisioned cannot be separated from managing the stresses and strains, the ups and down, the joys and sorrows of everyday life. The Christ centered holiness that Benedict envisioned comes about, with God's help, through ongoing conversion, through *ora et labora*, by participating in the daily offices, through the manner by which we accomplish even the simplest and meanest task *ad majorem gloria Dei*, and especially through the way we interact with others

---

[91]Rowan Williams, *Shaping Holy Lives*, Conference on Benedictine Spirituality, Holy Trinity, Wall Street, New York City, 29 April 2003. This lecture can be downloaded from www.archbishopofcanterbury.org

who no matter how different, difficult, and strange they may be, are our brothers and sisters beloved by the heavenly Father.

Balance, of course, requires stability. Without stability balance becomes impossible. Stability not only of place but also of spiritual practice, of avoiding extremes, of knowing and accepting one's own needs and limitations, of taking care of one's physical health, in short of developing holy habits. Regular spiritual practice, including time set aside for *hesychia* for contemplative silence, is a critically important part of such a stability.

Third, increasing self-awareness. Intentionally entering into silence, even for a brief time, is itself an experience of being in the desert for a while. We do not literally have to go to the desert to experience the desert. When seek contemplative silence, we soon find out what the Abbas and Ammas of old discovered, namely that when we seek silence to be closer to God and get away from the pressures of our life, from what they called the shipwreck of the world, the very first thing that happens is that we run into ourselves.

I have engaged in this practice long enough to know that there is a direct connection between slacking off from such contemplative practice and feeling more scattered and overburdened. In a fascinating doctoral thesis, Marilyn Pray, a Sister of St. Joseph in Rochester, New York, investigated the relationship between spirituality and burnout among those who minister in particularly trying circumstances, like ministry to the homeless and the multiply addicted. The conclusion was absolutely clear. Only those lasted who engaged in regular spiritual practice and were active members of a community of prayer and worship.[92]

I have discovered that the resistance many have to being silent is not only because it is associated in their minds with punishment, like solitary confinement or the age-old parental, "Go to your room!", but also because they are afraid of their own demons, of what they may encounter about themselves. "In the desert," the Greek Orthodox theologian Fr. John Chryssavgis writes, "you discover your true self, without any masks or myths. There [in the presence of God] you are forced to come to terms with yourself.

---

[92]Marilyn Pray, SSJ, *Journey of integration: the convergence of pastoral care of marginalized persons with the prophetic spirituality of the pastoral care giver.* Unpublished D. Min. Dissertation, Colgate Rochester Divinity School, 1996.

Ultimately, you are called to face up to and fight against the demons, without blaming someone else or your past."[93]

I have experienced more self-confrontation in practicing *hesychia* than in all the psychotherapy I have had. And in my training as a psychotherapist I have had quite a bit. The reason, I believe, is that with human therapists, no matter how skillful they are, it does not take long to figure out what they like to hear and to what they do not pay much attention. This makes it tempting to decide what to and what not to present. In contemplative prayer this is not possible. My experience has been that I know very well when I try to avoid the truth about myself before God. It is a humbling experience to become aware of playing games in prayer. It reveals a great deal about ourselves.

Abba Anthony the Great would approve. According to Abba Poemen he is reported to have said, 'this is the great work of a man: always to take the blame for his own sins before God and to expect temptation to this last breath.'"[94] It is important to remember that temptation for these Abbas and Ammas was not intrinsically negative, because it affords the opportunity for the critical spiritual practice of *apatheia*, of gaining control of one's conditioned impulses and responses. So the very next saying of Abba Anthony in the *The Sayings of the Desert Fathers* records that "He also said, 'Whoever has not experienced temptation cannot enter the Kingdom of Heaven.' He even added, 'Without temptations no one can be saved.'"[95] I have found this practical, humane, and hopeful approach to human infirmity of these ancient Christians enormously comforting and supportive.

Finally and most importantly, practicing the presence of Christ. My experience with churches and seminaries is that there is often more talk about God than reflection on experiences of God. This widespread objectification of faith that is evident in theological schools, in parishes and in dioceses is becoming increasingly problematic. As one New Testament scholar recently observed, "Learning about religion, theology, or spirituality may strengthen one's [sense of religious vocation], but it cannot substitute for the primary knowledge gleaned from one's own experience of the

---

[93] John Chryssavgis, *In the Heart of the Desert: The Spirituality of the Desert Fathers and Mothers* (World Wisdom, 2003) p. 37.
[94] *The Sayings of the Desert Fathers*, Abba Anthony #4, p. 2.
[95] *The Sayings of the Desert Fathers*, Abba Anthony #5, p. 2.

Holy'[96].

In retrospect, my own education, both secular and theological, imbued me with the conviction that the only legitimate ways in which truth can be known is through the mind and through the senses, that is to say through rational thought and through scientific research. It came as a revelation to me, not too many years ago, that there is a third way in which truth can be known, particularly truth about God, and that way is through the heart. How could I have missed that? Throughout Scripture and much of the Christian tradition until the last couple of hundred years, it was taken for granted that the heart is the centre of who we really are, for good or ill.

The heart not as the symbol of fuzzy, romantic love but as the mysterious and very real and alive place in and through which we can experience the Indwelling Spirit of our Lord. In a recent interview the Abbott of the Panagia[97] monastery in Cyprus put it this way, "Christ himself ... told us that not only are we capable of exploring God but that we can also live with Him, become one with Him. And the organ by which we can achieve this is neither our senses nor our logic but our heart."[98]

Does that mean we check our brains at the door? Of course not. We are bidden to love God with all our minds as well. Does that mean that theology is not important? Of course not. Without theology to guide us, direct us, instruct us, and help us see things we might otherwise not see, our spirituality would quickly become the privatized expression of our own wants and needs.

But it does mean that we need to practice standing prayerfully before God with the mind in the heart, to quote those well-known words of the 19th century Russian saint, Theophan the Recluse.[99] By this he meant that praying to God requires our intention, our mindful intention, to seek God, to listen to God, and to be open to the presence of Christ's indwelling Spirit in our hearts.

---

[96] L. William Countryman, *Living on the Border of the Holy: Renewing the Priesthood of All*, Morehouse (1999).

[97] *Panagia* means "Most Holy" and refers to the *Theotokos*, Mary the Mother of God.

[98] *The Mountain of Silence*, p. 43.

[99] *The Art of Prayer: An Orthodox Anthology*. Compiled by Igumen Chariton of Valamo, Translated by E. Kadloubovsky and E. M. Palmer, Edited with an introduction by Timothy Ware (Faber and Faber Paperback, 1997), p. 53. The faithful in St. Theophan's time prayed standing up.

All is Grace, but being aware of Christ's presence requires collaborative practice, the kind of practice that is indispensable if we are to acquire the mind of Christ. It is not an easy thing to do, for it requires commitment and ongoing conversion in the context of Christian community. When we look closely at the lives of men and women of faith throughout the Christian tradition, we find that for all their differences in culture, language, and the time in which they lived, it is evident that they, whether cloistered or in the world, were all grounded in that kind of spiritual practice, in what became known as *Contemplatio in Actione*, literally "contemplation in action" but which is best understood as "doing the work of Christ while grounded in Christ".

I mentioned earlier how surprised I was to realize that the most significant influences on my personal integration and priestly formation have been, and continue to be, the cultivation of *hesychia* through regular contemplative prayer, especially the Jesus Prayer, and a greater ability to understand and move through difficult times in my life from the perspective of purgation. Let me share a few tentative observations about these experiences.

Experience has shown me that purgation and *hesychia* can help, slowly but surely, to de-center the ego. Contrary to what I may have feared these experiences did not obliterate my ego or impaired my sense of self. On the contrary, they have imbued me with a more realistic sense of who I am. They have strengthened my identity. Neither have I experienced purgation and *hesychia* as an invitation to quietism, to a spiritual passivity that sits back in the hope that God will take care of things. On the contrary, it has made me more aware that the spiritual path cannot be engaged in halfheartedly but requires our best efforts.

At the same time I find myself less interested in successful outcomes than I used to be. What Anthony Bloom once said resonates with me. "What I aim at," he wrote, "is to live within a situation and to be totally engrossed in it and yet free from involvement ... The only question I keep asking myself in life is: what should I do at this particular moment? What should I say? All you can do is to be at every single moment as true as you can with all the power in your being - and then leave it to God to use you, even despite yourself."[100]

---

[100] Anthony Bloom (Metropolitan Anthony of Sourozh), *Beginning to Pray*

The practice of contemplative prayer has helped to me to trust more in the reality of God whether that presence is affectively felt or not. It has given me more freedom from the endemic forces of *emotivism* and materialism. Cultivating *hesychia* is helping me to move from abstraction to participation, from my head to my heart. This is slowly overcoming the disconnect that for so long has existed in me between theological abstraction and the reality of God and daily life.

Purgation and *hesychia* have also, again quite unexpectedly, contributed to the healing of memories. This has been a great blessing. Memories that have to do with traumatic experiences in my life, unresolved conflicts, missed opportunities, and many other burdens have kept my ego busy trying to resolve, overcome, and control even though such efforts rarely succeeded and usually only added to a sense of failure. The healing of memories is enormously liberating.

Purgation and *hesychia* have made me profoundly aware of the importance of authentic Christian community. In our weekly formation meetings at Bexley Hall Seminary we, both faculty and students, spend time sitting in contemplative silence together. It has confirmed the truth of what Simone Weil once said, "For nothing among human things has such power to keep our gaze fixed ever more intensely upon God, than friendship for the friends of God."[101] And it has taught me that solitude, learning to be by myself, is a prerequisite for being able to participate fully in community. Just as the ability to participate in community is needed for true solitude.

Finally, it has moved me to a more Christocentric understanding faith and ministry. It has made the Indwelling Spirit of our Lord more of a reality for me. It has made me much more aware than I used to be of our need to be grounded in this Spirit, and by doing so, to reflect that Spirit as best we can in our life and ministry.

PASTORES DABO VOBIS

More than a decade ago Pope John Paul II gave the title *Pastores Vobis Dabo*, meaning *Shepherds I Give You*, to his important *Apostolic Exhortation on the Formation of Priests*. This

---

(Paulist Press, 1970), p. 14.

[101]Simone Weil, *Waiting for God* (Harper Colophon Edition, 1973), p. 74.

title was taken from a passage in Jeremiah where, in a time of political uncertainty and turmoil much like ours, God promises his disheartened people, "I will give you shepherds after my own heart"[102], shepherds who would be there for them and with them so that God's people no longer would have to be afraid. In that same *Apostolic Exhortation* the Pope emphasized that, "The priest's fundamental relationship is to Jesus Christ, head and shepherd."[103]

I want to conclude this lecture by sharing an experience which, in an immediate and compelling way, helped me understand this fundamental relationship between our Lord as head and shepherd and the pastoral and priestly ministry to which we have been called. In the early 1990s I participated in a two year long program in spiritual direction at the Shalem Institute for Spiritual Formation in Bethesda, Maryland. During one of the several long retreats that were part of that program, I was introduced to praying with ikons. The retreat leader, Tilden Edwards,[104] told us about the rich tradition of ikons in the Eastern Orthodox Church and their role in liturgy and personal prayer.

He made clear that you do not pray to ikons but with ikons. The most important thing in an ikon, he pointed out, are its eyes. *"You pray with the ikon looking at yourself as if God were looking at you through the eyes of the ikon."* He had brought two famous ikons for our group to pray with, the *Vladimir Madonna* from the 12th century, the Blessed Virgin holding the infant Jesus, and a *Pantokrator Christ*, meaning "Christ the Ruler of All", an ikon from the 6th century, which can still be seen in the Monastery of St. Catherine on the Sinai peninsula.

The ikons had been set up on tables with chairs in front of them so that several people could sit and pray with one ikon at a time. Right away I felt strongly drawn to the *Sinai Pantokrator*. I had never seen a depiction of Jesus that I thought resembled what he may have actually looked like. I must admit that I felt a bit uneasy

---

[102]Jeremiah 3:15.

[103]Pope John Paul II, *Pastores Dabo Vobis: Post-Synodal Apostolic Exhortation on the Formation of Priests in the Circumstances of the Present*, 1992, Chapter 2, No. 16.

[104]The Rev. Tilden Edwards was at that time the Executive Director of thee Shalem Institute for Spiritual Formation, 5430 Grosvenor Lane, Bethesda, MD 20814, USA www.shalem.org

at first. I was raised in the Reformed tradition and worries about idolatry began to arise in my mind. But after a while I was able to let go of my anxiety, and I asked God to help me be open to the presence of the Spirit.

Remembering what Tilden had said about looking at yourself through the eyes of the ikon as if God were looking at you, I noticed that Jesus' right eye seemed to take everything in, very diagnostically, almost like an X-ray. And the left eye, with a faint tear trickling down our Lord's cheek, conveyed profound compassion. At that point something completely unexpected happened. I burst into tears. I had this strong sense of God seeing me through the eyes of this ikon of Jesus, seeing right through me, seeing all the parts of me that I was not proud of or felt badly about, all my sins and errors, but also seeing me with a look of incredible compassion, making me know that I was accepted, that I too am loved.

It was a profound moment in my spiritual journey. The experience with the *Sinai Pantokrator* showed me a more *hesychastic* way to pray. It taught me how to be more open to the presence of our Lord's spirit of compassion and truth which sees us for what we are, warts and all, but which also embraces us in healing love. That day I understood in a new and profound way how God knows me through and through and yet loves me.

This experience helped me know beyond a doubt that the goal of spiritual practice is to acquire the mind of Christ. This is not an easy time to be a priest or deacon but it helps me to remember that we are not called to be successful or victorious but to be faithful, to acquire the mind of Christ, to be his ikons in the world, and to reflect his compassion and truthfulness to all those with whom we come in contact.

May the faculty, students and graduates of Bovendonk continue to find their identity in Christ, may they move through good and bad times trusting Christ, may they know Christ through the experience of his presence, and may they be his ikons in the ministry to which they have been called.

Laus Deo!

Part III:

EVALUATION

10. BOVENDONK PROGRAMME: AN EVALUATION

By Jan Snijders

In the hope that you haven't heard it before, I would like to start by telling a story I first encountered at the Holbein Exhibition in The Hague. After the death of his third wife, Henry VIII sent his Chancellor Thomas Cromwell to find him another wife from among the noble families on the continent. Cromwell's choice fell on Anne of Cleves, and he instructed Hans Holbein, the official portrait painter at Henry's court, to produce a portrait of the intended bride. Holbein agreed, and he made Anne look so beautiful that Henry immediately fell head over heels in love with her. Henry then commanded her to come over by the first available ship; but when she arrived, he was so disappointed that he promptly sent her back again. The moral of the story is quite simple: don't make it any nicer than it really is. I'll try not to.

When the programme of priestly formation first began at Bovendonk twenty years ago, it attracted its fair share of patronising comment. As a product of the Tridentine system myself, and as a former lecturer in another seminary, I can well understand the implied superiority of the critics. But twenty years on, Bovendonk has not only survived, it has prepared 73 seminarians for ordination, or around one fifth of the total number of new priests in the Netherlands over that time. So, perhaps we can drop the *apologia*; Bovendonk no longer needs to justify itself. But there is no reason to repeat Holbein's mistake either.

The Tridentine model was built around two stages. The first was the minor seminary – in practice, a secondary boarding school for boys learning classical languages. This was followed by a six year residential programme at the main seminary designed exclusively for candidates to the priesthood. The syllabus was made up of two years philosophy followed by four years academic theology. The lectures were all given by resident staff, most of whom were also priests. This system has been extremely successful, and over the centuries since the Counter-Reformation, has supplied our church with an abundance of high calibre clergy - more than enough for the parishes and other forms of pastoral ministry and missionary activity. That must be said.

But if we look back further, behind the uniformity of the Tridentine system, we discover that the church had previously adopted a far more varied approach to priestly formation. Ignatius came from the military (one of the few professions not yet represented at Bovendonk!). Deacon Francis came from the cloth trade. Augustine, not such a bad bishop in the end, had been a university lecturer. One of the apostles worked for the Inland Revenue, and several others were fishermen. The Lord himself was a builder (Bovendonk prides itself on having had one builder).

The Council of Trent decided that the time was right for a more systematic approach. But this system, which over four centuries had been so successful and stable, collapsed in a matter of years nearly everywhere in Europe and beyond. The blame-game for this collapse will entertain those who enjoy passing the buck, but we won't go into that at the moment. The fact is, the program crashed.

Since then, there have been many attempts to tweak the system, not without success. But at the same time other forms of priestly formation have sprung up. One example is the pattern of maintaining a residential base for formation, but using the local university to provide the teaching. But perhaps the most radical alternative model is this one - a part-time programme which enables students to prepare for the priesthood alongside their existing professional commitments. And let me immediately add, not only priests - for several years now, Bovendonk has trained candidates for the diaconate from the dioceses of Breda and Rotterdam.

The Tridentine system also recognised the (so-called) 'late vocation'. But these candidates had to be very brave; they were men who, at the ripe old age of eighteen or twenty, were expected to sit in the back row of classes for twelve-year olds. Highly motivated and determined, they struggled with their studies, usually got little sympathy from either staff or students, but often became faithful priests and pastors. Occasionally, there were attempts to design specific programmes for this kind of candidate, but few people in practice were really that interested. There were enough candidates to fill the seminaries anyway.

But Bovendonk is something quite different. 'Mature student' in this place means a person who is at least thirty or forty years of age. A few are even older - the average age at ordination is actually 43. They have a career, and have often had a professional training before joining the course. Then, for the first four years, they continue to work alongside their part-time studies for the priesthood, attending twenty long week-ends every year.

Don't think this is a soft option. It means six years of countless weekends away, followed by sheer hard work during the week while friends and colleagues enjoy family life, sports or hobbies. The classes are only the tip of the iceberg; for every topic taught over a week-end you must remember the two hours preparation during the week. If you decide to reduce your working hours – assuming that is even an option – your income will drop. Some have even had to sell their property. Even telling your colleagues you are studying for the priesthood can be an anxious experience. All in all, it takes utter determination!

When I first started to teach here 15 years ago, the students were mostly men who had started in a classical seminary when they were younger, but had given up for one reason or another. This is no longer the case.

Quite a few of the present students had effectively opted out of the church and religion for years, perhaps not attending at all. Quite a few therefore have returned because they have been through a personal conversion. This means they are highly motivated, as shown by the fact that few students at Bovendonk ever miss a weekend. Many students have been moved by the dramatic shortage of priests, or by the spiritual poverty they encounter in the community. Sadly, the odd student can occasionally be heard talking dismissively about the modern world, but these are very much the exception, and Bovendonk usually succeeds in curing them of such disdain! Most of the students are not *innovators* bent on changing everything in the Church. They may have their reservations about one thing or the other, but they usually handle such things in a mature way. They are here to serve.

The practical advantages of this formula are obvious. First of all the students continue to earn their living. Bread on the table without becoming dependent is for practical as well as psychological reasons important for men who for years have stood on their own two feet.

Equally important is the opportunity to explore the idea of priestly vocation without first having to give up your job or interrupt your career. And the advantage is two-way: dioceses also get to know candidates and test their suitability before they burn their boats. One way or another, this gives both sides a refreshing degree of freedom for a substantial period of time.

Opinions will differ about the usefulness of this freedom. Some people will argue that this does not create the right conditions for the radical and definitive decision every priest must make sooner or later. Personally, I feel most people these days need a long time to consider far-reaching decisions of this kind, and this lengthy lead-in time therefore improves the quality of the final decision considerably. Others argue that some candidates are already ready to make a commitment, so why postpone it? In the Netherlands, most dioceses in practice opt for one side or another. But the question needs to be asked whether or not a more sensible approach might be to tailor formation to reflect the psychological and spiritual condition of each individual candidate.

The Bovendonk approach has disadvantages. The idea of living in community for several years in a seminary or a diocesan house enables candidates to establish strong personal links with the diocese and with fellow students. More attention can perhaps be given to what is sometimes called a "diocesan spirituality", though as a religious I am not quite sure what that might mean.

Further, a part-time framework means that Bovendonk students invest far less time in academic study than would be the case in a classical seminary or university course. The theory is that prior professional learning compensates for this shortfall, though it would be useful to find out whether this is in fact the case. There is little doubt, though, that some of the 'late vocations' in the early days came into training with so much excess baggage that they did not show a great deal of evidence of learning from experience. Maybe this also highlights the merits of deciding on full-time or part-time training on a case-by-case basis.

No one starts at Bovendonk as a *tabula rasa*. Everyone starts with a great deal of prior learning; Teachers know how to handle young people - how they react, how they think, how to pass on knowledge and values. Important skills for a future pastor. Male nurses know how to deal with the sick or the elderly. They know how to approach them pastorally, better than those who stand at the sick-bed as mere visitors. Very important also. So perhaps it is worth noting that the majority of candidates in Bovendonk come from the teaching or nursing professions.

Other professions may have less obvious links with parochial ministry. A bricklayer's skill may not be immediately useful in pastoral work, although other builders in the parish might enjoy having a pastor who knows something about their work. The first carpenter priest got most of his parables from farming and fishing rather than his own building trade – apart, that is, from the faulty estimates of the tower and the corner stone (borrowed from the psalm!).

Important too are the collaborative skills learnt in any profession: consulting, the give and take of team dynamics, learning to live and work with people of different opinions and attitudes.

Even so, the heart of the matter, in my view, lies not in specific professional skills but in the fact that for years the candidate has functioned in the everyday secular world, and continues to do so while studying theology. This is crucial, in my view. As a result, the academic assignments set between teaching weekends need to avoid the danger of overloading the student. Lecturers from the academic world may be tempted to pile it on, but part of the role of the Rector and the Dean of Studies is to prevent this from happening. The combination of work and study must remain 'double'.

But the theological learning started at weekends lives on in the mind and experience of the candidate as he returns to his job, and as he continues to wrestle with these ideas in the context of regular contact with the views and the attitudes of people at work. At the same time, these views and attitudes are taken back when he returns to study. I often have been struck by the ease with which students take my familiar theological jargon and translate it instantly into everyday language. I remember one student who, after listening to me dutifully, simply said 'they'll never buy that on our factory floor'. He got a good mark straightaway.

The same applies to the process of personal conversion that is even more important than theology on the journey towards ordination. Surely this process involves periods of withdrawal. Whoever wants to follow the Lord has to do his forty days in the desert. But it may actually help men to go through this desert experience in the very secular context in which the priest will find himself in ministry. Trees need strong roots during a storm. Standing up to the storm is a demanding spiritual exercise, however, so perhaps that is another question that needs to be considered on a case-by-case basis.

That theology has its own jargon does not matter (and theologians love it). Any scholarly discipline has its own language. But when this jargon interferes with the proclamation of the Gospel it certainly does matter. I fear we do not recognise clearly enough how far the language of the Word is removed from the people we are called to serve. I remember an elderly lady who with great interest read the *Catechism of the Catholic Church* and then lent the book to her daughter, a General Practitioner who had lost contact with the Church. After a few weeks she got the *Catechism* back with the comment: "Mum, just the book for you; personally, I don't understand a word of it". To be fair, I recently heard someone say exactly the same thing about the famous so-called 1966 Dutch catechism!

Thirty-five years ago, Willem van de Pol announced the end of what he provocatively called 'conventional Christianity'. Fortunately, his announcement proved to be somewhat premature, and countless examples of this 'conventional Christianity' survive happily in many a parish. It is astonishing how much energy and money goes into restoring barely-used parish churches, (especially!) when the diocese has decided to close the building. In Banneux, I once saw more Dutch number plates than all the other cars put together. Lourdes can barely handle the number of pilgrims. And on the occasion of the hundred and fiftieth jubilee of the restoration of the hierarchy in our country it looked for a moment as if the former Catholic life-style would flower once again on renewed soil. Sorry, Willem, conventional Christianity is stronger than you think.

The familiar parish ministry of Sunday services, funerals, marriages, baptisms and visiting the sick will therefore continue to fill the life of the priest trained at Bovendonk. Those beautiful words *pastorate* and *pastoral,* or the archaic expression *cure of souls* somehow makes me think of the poet Guido Gezelle.

An interesting question is how do the priests who were trained in Bovendonk actually survive in pastoral ministry? Can they cope?

As they look back, what do they think about their formation? How do the parishes and dioceses see it? I do not know the answer, and I doubt if anyone can do more than relate isolated anecdotes. I once suggested that we need a systematic study of outcomes from the Bovendonk programme. I know our Church has not yet adopted with Karl Popper's notion of an *Open Society*, but I am sure it should be possible to find a sympathetic sociologist who will respect the privacy of all those concerned, yet also help the Bovendonk community to learn from twenty years of experience.

Willem van de Pol is not entirely wrong, of course - how could he, such a learned man. While many elements of conventional Christianity happily live on inside and outside the Church, lots of people brought up as Catholics nevertheless keep themselves at a safe distance from their spiritual inheritance. Most of them would still be counted among the figure of 5,060,000 Catholics given in the *Pius Almanak* of 2000. But less than 10% of those five million Catholics regularly attend Mass; twenty years ago it would have been 23%. Less than half of them get married in church, and one third of their children are not baptised. And, as Haarsma has put it, the teaching of the Church often has little in common with the *de facto* belief and practices of her members.

Yet, these five million nominal Catholics represent no more than one third of the people of our country. How many others have not even heard the name of the Lord? Sometimes I am reminded of the prophet Jonah and his moaning about that ridiculous bush, and the Lord's rebuke: should I not grieve for Nineveh, the secular city (my translation), with all those people, to say nothing about the animals. And our pastors are already overburdened!

It is now more than ten years since our Church was challenged to become missionary as well as pastoral. It was a bit of a shock at the time. I don't know why, because we had been told for over half a century that France is now a *pays de mission*. It was our national pride, perhaps, that fed the illusion that God was doing rather better in Holland than France. But now we have got used to the idea - so much so, that some people even speak of *missionary parishes*. A bridge too far, in my opinion, if that is meant to suggest that mission can be left to our dear greying congregations. Instead, I think it would be a significant step forward if we started to understand that mission simply needs to be put on the same professional footing as traditional pastoral ministry.

You may remember what happened when the American media bishop Fulton Sheen returned from the first session of Vatican II and met with a group of faithful Irish Catholics in New York. His audience anxiously enquired 'Surely, Bishop, what we read in the papers can't be true - that there were serious differences of opinion between the bishops at the Council?' 'Dear people', said the bishop, 'You know that the Lord sometimes likened his disciples to shepherds, sometimes to fishermen. Well, I can tell you one thing: shepherds and fishermen are two very different sorts of people. They do not speak the same language, and sometimes they have difficulty understanding each other.'

As far as I am aware, nobody has yet written a missionary theology designed to address the needs of the secularised world, but it is time to put this right. I'll throw in a few ideas for starters. The missionary task is not simply a variation of pastoral care. Nor is it an extension of pastoral work. It belongs in a class of its own; it is *sui generis*.

To name just one distinctive aspect of mission: it takes a long time, and moves like a glacier, without what one cynical French missiologist called the urge for *rentabilité sacramentaire.* I am reminded of an old Irish sister teaching in what was almost exclusively a Muslim girls' school in the heart of Pakistan, who told me she was now teaching the granddaughters of the girls she had taught when she first arrived, half a century earlier. I cautiously asked her if she saw a difference. She smiled proudly and said 'Oh yes, Father; they have mellowed beautifully'.

Then there is the Worker Priest in a very de-Christianized industrial town in central France. He had worked on the assembly line of a truck factory for ten years without anybody realising he was a priest, until the day one of his fellow workers attended a funeral he conducted on a Saturday. By Monday morning, the word was out. At first, everybody avoided him. Then one of the roughest characters came up and said, 'Is it true, *tu es curé?* You are a priest?' 'Yes', he said, 'didn't you know?' 'Well', said the fellow, 'we are happy to know. And now we also know that not all priests are 'rogues''. In fact he used another word, but that one is not in the dictionary.

I have already put the question, how well have Bovendonk priests performed in on-going pastoral ministry, without the benefit of a more academic university course or full-time residence in a traditional seminary. Now another question: if you are required on a daily basis to integrate your theology into the secular reality of your ordinary job, could it be that you are better prepared for the missionary dimension of priesthood? Safely distant from the secular world, theology and preaching can sound delightfully wonderful. You can persuade yourself you both understand and are understood, only to discover later - or even worse, not discover at all - that you were actually entirely out of your depth.

Could it be, therefore, that Bovendonk has something important to say about developing missionary skills and a missionary spirituality? And, following that, does Bovendonk exploit these missionary possibilities as fully as it might through its teaching and supervision? In Fulton Sheen's words, does it in fact produce fishermen as well as shepherds?

This makes me think of a painting which is well-known in a local Sanatorium for Lepers on one Pacific island. A gifted leper painted a vast mural with his deformed fingers showing the arrival of the first missionaries as he imagined it. In the foreground, the dominating figure of a missionary in a black cassock and holding up a large cross steps out of a boat on the beach, whilst a long line of local people back away looking utterly dumbfounded. But as the viewer looks closely along the line of men, women and children, they see one man with a lighter complexion (that is, a leper) who holds a small cross behind his back. The mural has no text, and no words are needed. You can only stand still in front of the picture and feel very humble.

In the good old days, priests met their people through familiar parish structures. With the faithful parishioners of today, this pattern lives on. But a growing majority of people no longer live in the terraced houses of the parish. Instead of the orderly and uniform parish communities of former times, there is now a bewildering variety of ways people can relate, or fail to relate, to the Church and to the faith. Official statistics show only what I have called the terraced houses in the parish; the rest have slipped out of the familiar categories and quietly disappeared.

Just think of:

- members of the choir who come to church only when they sing,
- volunteers who limit their commitment to specific tasks (I know of at least one church member whose membership amounts to cutting the grass),
- the independent groups, often with an intensive spiritual life of their own, but lacking any formal connection with the parish or diocese.

In an article in the Newsletter of the Mariënburgvereniging, Kees Waaijman recently described the very different starting-points of contemporary spirituality:

- bodily experience,
- internal experience of divine presence
- social engagement
- interreligious and ecumenical contacts

One might also add:

- ecology and the environment
- political involvement.

And then there are the countless people who live as nomads in the spiritual desert of our highly individualized world. They will never again feel at home in the terraced houses of the parish. At most, the Church offers them only an oasis, a place to stop when they feel the need, and from which they will leave as soon as the need has gone. A priest needs a real missionary spirituality to allow the Church to become such an oasis. So the challenge is this: how can we nurture *this* kind of spirituality?

I have suggested that all this takes patience. It takes the long view, the capacity to travel with the nomads however far their journey has taken them. Not, like the missionary in the leper's mural, eager to overwhelm the locals with a message they cannot hear, but to search for the hidden Lord who is already with them travelling unseen. Or, in the words of Clement of

Alexandria, quoted at the II Vatican Council, looking for the *semina verbi,* the seeds of the Word, sown everywhere by the great Sower who went out to sow (Mt 13,3; *Ad Gentes,*11).

This is what Bovendonk can and must mean - the unique opportunity to prepare for missionary ministry. Studying for ordination whilst remaining in daily contact with work colleagues, contemplating God's Word whilst continuing in secular life, cannot fail to draw attention to the *semina verbi.* Learning to care for the community where one lives and works can foster a profound appreciation for those going through the wilderness of life, and for the anonymous cross each person must carry. You come to like ordinary people, and you come to like the world in which you both live. I still remember the Oblate Father who once told me: if you want to work in the North of Canada, you must like snow and you must like Eskimos.

This is the task Bovendonk set itself twenty years ago. This is, I think, the mission Bishop Ernst gave to Bovendonk when he established this institution. This is the direction students and lecturers have sought to follow for all these years. May Bovendonk always get the support it deserves. May it continue to make a contribution to the Church as a pastoral and missionary agency of the reign of God.

11. BOVENDONK – ANOTHER PATH TO PRIESTHOOD
By Kevin Rafferty

On a summer's evening in early June of this year I arrived in the small Dutch village of Hoeven, just over the Belgian border into the Netherlands. I had travelled the 15 kilometres west from Breda, through the flat Dutch countryside with its rows of trees, cultivated fields and well kept houses. After passing the parish church in the middle of the village I drove up a beautiful tree lined avenue to an imposing seminary building.

I was to discover later that this seminary had been designed by a famous Dutch architect, Petrus Cuypers, who had also designed the ornate Central Railway Station and the Rijksmuseum in Amsterdam at the end of the 19th century. The façade of this building was no less ornate. This seminary had served generations of priests in the Diocese of Breda for over 100 years. Waiting at the door to greet me was the Rector, Fr Matthias Ham. Over the next few days I was to learn more about a very interesting approach to seminary formation which may have something to teach us in our European context in the years ahead.

Beginnings

In the turbulent post Vatican II years Bovendonk seminary, like its counterparts in other parts of the Netherlands, came to an abrupt end. In 1967 all existing seminaries (over 30) in the country were closed overnight. The leadership in the Dutch Catholic Church had come to the conclusion that seminaries, as they existed, were no longer appropriate places to prepare students for priesthood. The numbers of students entering seminaries over these years was rapidly declining.

There needed to be some rationalisation of the 30 existing centres of formation - diocesan seminaries and theologates of religious orders. It was agreed that from now on five theological centres in Utrecht, Tilburg, Nijmegen, Heerlen and Amsterdam, would provide for the theological needs of seminarians in the Netherlands. Seminarians would live in small Christian communities or in religious houses. These centres would also provide for the increasing number of lay students who wanted to study theology and to prepare for the exercise of various ministries including that of 'pastoral worker' now opening up in the Dutch Catholic Church.

Over the following twenty years these centres had varying degrees of success. In 1973 the bishop of Roermond reopened his seminary and ran it along traditional lines amidst a good deal of controversy about the quality of students and the kind of formation on offer there.

In 1983, Msgr. Hubertus Ernst, bishop of Breda, decided to open the doors of the diocesan seminary at Bovendonk once again to candidates for the priesthood. When the seminary had closed in 1967 it had been purchased by a property developer who had built houses on the extensive grounds. However because the seminary itself was listed on the national registry as a historic building he could not get permission to develop it as he had planned. The building had remained vacant for ten years.

The grounds belonging formerly to the seminary became a public park and the seminary building was sold back to the diocese for the princely sum of 1 guilder and was used as a retreat/conference centre. These activities have continued in Bovendonk right up to the present day. Despite the ten year period of non-use the building was still in reasonably good condition and it was this building Msgr. Ernst decided to use as a training centre for a new kind of seminary.

In the 1980s Bishop Ernst had observed that many people in their middle years were changing their occupations and professions. It dawned on him that some of these people might be interested in priesthood. So he decided to follow through on this idea and he reopens the seminary in Bovendonk on a new kind of footing. After being closed as a seminary for 16 years Msgr. Ernst realised that by widening his horizons on the nature of seminary formation he had a use and a need for this beautiful building once again.

In doing this he was influenced by a seminary for 'late vocations 'which had operated in Antwerp, over the border in Belgium. However what Msgr. Ernst had in mind was going to be somewhat different.

A Non-Residential Seminary

Instead of bringing candidates together in a residential setting he decided to leave these candidates at their place of work and asked them to commute to Bovendonk at weekends from Friday evening to Sunday lunchtime for lectures, tutorials and seminars. So while remaining at work these students attended 21 weekends in Bovendonk each year for four years, covering the essentials of theology, philosophy and spirituality.

After the first year, if the students could negotiate it, they could cut down their work commitments to four days each week, using the extra day to read in the library and to prepare their coursework assignments. However, having a job and holding on to it was a condition for entry into the training programme.

Another condition of acceptance was that they be either active members of their parish communities or a member of a religious congregation. Since the 1960s many forms of both voluntary and salaried lay ministry had developed in the Netherlands. It was taken for granted that to be a member of a Christian community, be it a parish or some other group, one committed ones talents and gifts to building up and supporting this community. One could say that this active involvement in their parish communities was a first stage on their road to priesthood.

The four years participation in weekend seminars was a second stage in this path towards priesthood. The courses in scripture, theology and related subjects opened up their minds to the riches of the Catholic theological tradition. Matt Ham did not deny that attending these 21 week-ends each year over four years put a good deal of pressure on the students. He pointed out that the weekend seminars provided an interesting contrast to the other kinds of work they were engaged in during the week.

In the fifth and sixth year students gave up their jobs, took up residence in parishes and worked full time in the parishes they were assigned to. They continued to attend Bovendonk at weekends to cover various aspects of pastoral theology. A mentoring process which included pastoral-theological reflection and supervision in groups of 3 students was put in place to monitor every aspect of their initiation into parish ministry. Half way through the 6th year they were ordained to the diaconate at Bovendonk and at the end of the 6th year they were ordained to priesthood in their own diocese.

Having looked carefully at the content of the curriculum for the first four years of this course I was amazed at the amount of theology, biblical studies, and related subjects that were covered on this in-service basis over the 21 weekends each year. As far as I could see the essentials of the *Ratio Fundamentalis* were covered but at what depth it was difficult to say. The students had to work intensively to keep up with the range of courses on offer and to complete the course work requirements.

I got the impression that a range of adult education methodologies were being used. The programme was an intensive one and there must have been a good deal of pressure on these students to stay the course and maintain their professional work commitments. Built into the week-ends were times for prayer and Eucharist as well as time for socialising in which students had opportunities to get to know one another. Students were also members of various committees - liturgical, social, etc to look after various aspects of the weekend workshops and to promote their lives as students preparing for priestly and diaconate ministries.

Faculty

Apart from the Rector himself who lives in the seminary and the Director of Studies, a layman, the faculty are part-time and come to the seminary at weekends on a visiting basis. They are carefully selected to fit in with the aims of the seminary and to communicate a theology with a focus on Christian living and also to work closely with the students to help them to integrate their theology courses with their experience. A number of them come from various orders and congregations of men and women, bringing with them a variety of charisms and spiritualities.

A good deal of attention is paid to the human development of students and for this reason each student has a counsellor whom he meets on a fortnightly basis right through their six year programme. Particular attention is paid to the integration of theology with one's life experiences and also to a student's psychosexual development.

Matthias Ham himself completed his own training as a psychologist in Rome at the Gregorian University's Institute of Psychology. He brings a good deal of the expertise and skills he acquired there to bear on the human development of students and their motivation for wanting to be ordained priests or deacons. I gathered from our conversations that there was a strong emphasis on the human development of students and how this related to other aspects of formation - spiritual, intellectual and pastoral.

Matthias Ham saw it as his task to make sure that the variety of models of human development his staff members were using were not in conflict with one another. One priority the faculty shared was to avoid any kind of dualism – separation of spirituality from life experiences. Staff members were carefully chosen so that they could assist students on the road to personal integration.

Matthias Ham has held the post of Rector for the last 10 years. He himself has an interesting background. As a young man he emigrated to Brazil. After a few years he entered a seminary there, commuting from a parish base to attend lectures each morning, and completed his seminary training against a background of the intense efforts of the Brazilian bishops to communicate the riches of the Second Vatican Council to both priests and lay men and women.

He missed out on all the polarisation of church groups in the Netherlands. He was familiar with a Latin American situation where there was a grave shortage of priests. In Brazil a small percentage of the then 160 million Catholics come to church on a regular basis. The current 7% practice rate among Catholics in the Netherlands is similar to what he had experienced in Brazil.

There was also a situation in Brazil where 80% of the services on a Sunday were conducted by laity, 80% of whom were women. In contrast to the Netherlands he remarked that priests in Brazil were reasonably sure of their identity and roles as priests. Laymen and women were also conscious of their roles in both church and society not as auxiliaries of priests but with their own distinctive vocations as lay men and women.

Matthias Ham lives easily with the notion of a variety of seminaries or theologates to respond to the needs of different kinds of students. Those who are interested in academic theology are able to go to university departments of theology such as Utrecht, Tilburg or Nijmegen.

I learned that Neo-Catechumenate seminaries have opened their doors in two Dutch dioceses, that of Haarlem and Roermond. There is a plan under discussion to develop a Pontifical University in the city of Utrecht.

Matthias Ham was proud of the achievements of Bovendonk. Between 1983 and 2004 75 priests had been ordained, the majority of whom were diocesan priests. A quarter of those ordained belonged to religious orders or congregations. There was very little post ordination fall out and the fall out of students during their six years of formation was about 37% - a figure well below the usual fall out figure of 50% or more which we hear about today.

In its first year of foundation, 1983, 17 men were selected out of 28 applicants and enrolled in Bovendonk. This number grew gradually to 47 in the 1990s. However in recent years the annual enrolment has fallen back to the twenties. A great range of professional backgrounds are represented – health care workers, teachers, a lawyer, a baker, a builder, local government officials, and so on.

There is also a great range of intellectual backgrounds – from those with the equivalent of university entrance to those with higher professional qualifications. Some find the academic requirements of the course too demanding and drop out. Students make a contribution to the cost of the course but dioceses and religious congregations cover 80% of the fees.

Pastores Dabo Vobis

On a number of occasions during our conversations Matt touched on the fact that he was operating inside the framework of *Pastores Dabo Vobis* and especially the opportunities opened up by the famous paragraph 64. It is interesting to note that the authors of *Pastores Dabo Vobis* confirmed Canon Law which let the door open for the radical step taken in Bovendonk in 1983. The following is a quotation from Paragraph 64 of that document:

"We should also mention the phenomenon of priestly vocations arising among people of adult age, after they have spent some years as lay men working in various professions. This phenomenon is not new in the history of the Church. Today such vocations are more frequent and have some new features. It is not always possible, and often it is not even to be recommended, that these students be asked to follow the formation programme of the Major Seminary."

Rather, after a careful discernment of the genuineness of such vocations, what needs to be provided is some kind of specific programme of formation for them, especially adapted to their needs. In this way one ensures that they receive the spiritual and intellectual formation they need. One will also need to provide opportunities for these students to relate to other candidates for the priesthood and to spend some periods of time in the community of the Major Seminary. This can be a way of guaranteeing that such vocations are fully inserted into the one presbyterate.

If it is true that the declining numbers of students entering seminaries today in the western world is predominantly of students who are in a much older age group than 18 year old school leavers perhaps what is happening in a place like Bovendonk should be considered more and more as the norm for today in western Europe rather than the exception. The old pattern of students proceeding straight to seminaries after leaving secondary school is disappearing in many parts of Europe.

There are good psychological reasons for postponing entry into seminaries of whatever kind until later. At the age of 18 many people are still trying to find themselves and they are not in a position to make an initial commitment to a way of life such as priesthood. Of course there are exceptions. One could also argue that making even this initial commitment presupposes an adult conversion to Christianity which for many people comes later, often as a result of a crisis in their personal or professional lives.

Some Observations and Questions

Over the next few weeks I had plenty of time to reflect on what I had learned in Bovendonk. I also had an opportunity to talk with Matthias Ham later in the summer when he visited me in Dublin for a few days. The following are a number of observations and questions that occurred to me:

Students make a decision gradually over a four year period:

The fact that students remain in a work situation means that the decision for priesthood is a gradual one. Over a four year period they are able to explore this calling with the help of a Spiritual Director instead of making what may appear to be a once and for all decision to enter a residential seminary. This fits in very much with the mentality of many of our contemporaries who often find it difficult to make a once and for all decision which the giving up of their jobs might imply. They discover gradually if this calling to be a priest resonates with what is deepest within themselves. In this approach there is a much more realistic appreciation of the nature of a religious vocation as the slow dawning of a consciousness of a call from God to use one's talents and gifts in a particular way for the promotion of God's kingdom.

Students remain in a work situation:

In working in seminaries for a period of time one becomes aware of students who want to nestle in the seminary. Having to earn one's livelihood like everybody else keeps these students in Bovendonk rooted in reality. This also means that the theology and philosophy they study at week-ends has to pass the test of contact with everyday realities if it is to make sense for the students themselves and people they are interacting with in their work situations. The challenge of remaining at work and continuing to exercise a profession rules out many forms of escapism.

There is also a lot to be said for their remaining close to the local Christian communities that nurtured them in the first place. Perhaps it is there that one would expect them to receive a good deal of the support and encouragement they need if they are to persevere on this road to priesthood.

Training to be leaders:

Bringing students together in a residential situation for a six or seven year period may not be the only way to test a vocation or to find out if students have leadership capabilities. There are more direct ways these days to discover if they have or have not leadership potential and whether or not they can relate easily to men and women of our time. Today when students are coming from older age groups the traditional seminary environment may inhibit the genuine human and spiritual development of some students.

Integrating Theology and Life:

There is a good deal of emphasis on one to one tutorial work in Bovendonk. Students are encouraged to integrate the theology they are taught from week to week with their own personal experience. An effort is made to counteract any kind of dualism - keeping the world of theology and their own personal lives in watertight compartments. Students are challenged to integrate what they are learning about the Christian tradition with their own spiritual journeys and of course if they do this they are in a position to help others to do the same.

I was impressed by the practical steps which were being taken in Bovendonk to bring this about. A one hour counselling session every two weeks with each student by a staff member, with spiritual and psychological skills, is an integral part of the formation programme. Over the six years a student can have a variety of counsellors - men and women, priests and lay, theologians and experienced pastors.

In Year 5 and Year 6 this counselling process moves into an apprenticeship mode. During these two years students are placed in parishes where their pastoral work is carefully monitored. The two year placement in a parish in Year 5 and Year 6 is seen very much as a mentoring process to learn the pastoral skills they need to communicate with men and women. To some extent one could say that this is to return to an apprenticeship model of seminary formation which existed before the Tridentine seminary was set up.

The weekend workshops continue in Bovendonk where students have opportunities to reflect on and discuss what they are observing in the parishes they have been assigned to.

Psychosexual Development:

A good deal of attention is paid to the psychosexual development of these students. This is done through one to one counselling with counsellors in the first two years of their course. In this context one has to learn from the lessons of the past in which seminaries paid very little attention to this aspect of formation, leading to break down of one kind or another after students were ordained.

More and more today we have to face up to the limitations of an all male environment in promoting the psychosexual development of students. I could sense that in Bovendonk the staff members were doing their best to create a trusting environment in which students could attend to issues in their own psychosexual development and remove obstacles that could impede their ministry in the future.

Does Bovendonk go far enough?

In Bovendonk there were no students preparing for lay ministry. Bovendonk was restricted to men - those preparing for celibate priesthood and to deacons preparing for permanent diaconate ministry in the Roman Catholic tradition. Even in the present dispensation I felt that the place would be enriched if it opened its doors to lay men and women preparing for non ordained ministry on an in-service basis. There is no better way for seminarians to learn more about the gifts of lay men and women than to be sharing a classroom situation with them and becoming aware of the talents and gifts that they bring to a variety of ministries.

An important part of their ministry as priests in the future will be in helping men and women to discern their gifts and talents and encouraging them to use these gifts to build up Christian communities and so to prepare the way for collaborative ministry. With the diminishing number of priests in western European countries this collaboration is the only way parish communities will be able to continue. In the Netherlands at present there are other theological centres where pastoral workers are educated. The Bovendonk faculty have made a clear-cut option to concentrate on formation of priests and deacons and all their energies go into that. Theological, political and financial reasons have a part to play in that decision.

What kind of ecclesiology underpins the theology of priesthood in Bovendonk?

Over the few days I was in the Netherlands, I discovered that quite a variety of ecclesiologies could be encountered from one situation to another. Although polarisation between different groups in the Dutch Catholic Church seems to have diminished I could not help feeling that there was still a good deal of variation from one diocese to the next and indeed from one parish to the neigbouring one. In some situations what could be called a 'high 'theology of church prevailed. In other situations a 'low' theology of church predominated.

After visiting Bovendonk I was left wondering how this seminary was preparing its students to cope with this in the Dutch context. What became clear to me is that Bovendonk saw itself as approaching theology with a firm intention of remaining true to what was deepest in the Roman Catholic tradition. It distanced itself from the 'Religious Studies' approach of some of the University Departments of Theology. It also distanced itself from any narrow confessional or sectarian approach to theology which some extreme conservative groups were advocating.

Building up an esprit de corps

Every profession tries to promote an *esprit de corps*. Is the short period together sufficient for these students to develop an identity as a community of priests? As I walked through this seminary of Bovendonk I was impressed by the seminary itself as a building and the photographs of ordination classes of the past hanging on the walls reminded me that the seminary had a proud tradition of priestly formation.

It was in fact a very attractive set of buildings built around a courtyard with an impressive chapel at one end of that courtyard and an attractive dining-room and library on each side of the square. The groups of priests who had been ordained here in the past had experienced a distinctive kind of formation which must have helped them to bond together. What about this new generation? Are they bonding together and how do they relate to the older group of priests?

The Dutch context today

The last forty years have been difficult ones for the Dutch Catholic Church. After the euphoric days of the 1960s - the days of the publication of the so called Dutch Catechism, vibrant student liturgies, especially in the university chaplaincies, and the pioneering days of the Dutch Pastoral Council in which new structures were put in place for laity, priests and bishops, there followed a long period of conflict. The appointment of a number of extremely conservative bishops who could not hold the middle ground polarised the Dutch Catholic Church to a degree that alienated many Catholics.

At present the Dutch Catholic Church has moved into calmer waters. It is said that the 7 to 10% who are participating actively in the life of the church are very committed. The younger generation are no longer carrying the baggage of the post Vatican II conflicts. It is interesting to note that at present there are around 90 students preparing for priesthood in a variety of contexts, including Bovendonk.

Conclusion

Over the last ten years the conviction has grown in my mind that in Western Europe we are looking for new ways to call people to priestly ministry and we are looking for new ways to prepare them for this ministry in our secularised societies. I have become more and more convinced that what we call the Tridentine seminary, even in its most updated form, is not able to measure up to this challenge in our western world. There are certain ingredients in the Bovendonk seminary that point to a way forward:

- Belonging to and maintaining a strong link with one's parish community where there are possibilities of deepening one's life as a Christian.
- Remaining in a work context as the decision for priesthood grows and matures.
- Introducing a mentoring process or an apprenticeship structure for a significant part of the formation programme.

- Concentrating on a theology that has a practical orientation and is strongly focussed on communication with our contemporaries.
- Using a variety of human development processes and adult education methodologies.

For many years now we have been talking about the need for new forms of evangelisation in what we sometimes call 'Old Europe'. In this kind of context it is important that we begin to think beyond the framework of the traditional Tridentine seminary. This is why I found my brief visit to Bovendonk so interesting. Bovendonk points up a few ways to begin thinking creatively about new paths to priesthood in our western European context.

Printed in Great Britain
by Amazon